TRUE
WILD WEST
ON THE
COLORADO
PLAINS

Susan Eldringhoff

ISBN: 1500399760
ISBN 13: 9781500399764

CONTENTS

CONTENTS

INTRODUCTION:

"True Wild West on the Colorado Plains" is a series of short stories of real crimes, mysteries, and adventures that took place on the eastern plains of Colorado, beginning in the late nineteenth century up through the late twentieth century. I'm sure this barely scratches the surface of all the 'Wild West' tales that have taken place in this region. There were many other stories that have been passed down through the generations in which too few facts were known to even begin to dig for the truth. Other adventures, unfortunately, have just been lost to time.

When I started out, I wanted to write something about the history in Eastern Colorado, because most books, stories, movies, etc. dealing with Colorado history are about the early days of the mining camps and boom towns in the mountains. Most people think Colorado is all mountains anyway, so I wanted to tell some history of the Colorado Plains, which make up almost half the state.

My main objective was to find the truth of historical events, through research, and record them so they will be preserved for future generations, rather than lost to time. It deals, in most cases, with forgotten events and unknown people never before written about. They are not necessarily about famous or well known characters, but rather, ordinary citizens, or in some cases, ordinary criminals, who were all just trying to survive on the Colorado Plains.

What they all have in common is that they each got caught up in newsworthy events which made the newspapers of the day. A lot of my initial research was done in old Colorado newspapers. Most articles were short on details concerning the people involved. I tried to fill in the gaps, through many other avenues, whenever possible, but sometimes came to dead ends.

I hope the book conveys just how hard life was for our pioneer ancestors. How real life differed from typical movie westerns. Also, how the facts sometimes differ from the stories that have been passed down through folklore.

WHERE THE STORY BEGINS

The Settling of the West

There were Indian wars going on in Eastern Colorado long before the white man arrived. The predominant tribe that lived in this area in semi-recent history (eighteenth century) were the Apaches. From that time until the arrival of white settlers, many tribes fought each other for hunting territories. The Comanche and Shoshone tribes moved south from Wyoming. The Utes moved out of Utah to the Colorado Rockies and then pushed on down onto the plains. The Pawnee, and Wichita came in from Kansas. The Sioux even moved into northeastern Colorado in the early nineteenth century.

By the mid-nineteenth century, when the frontiersmen began arriving in greater numbers, the area was dominated by the Cheyenne and Arapaho who had moved in from the northern Great Plains.

Early in the nineteenth century, white trappers established fort-like trading posts to trade with the Indians. Bent's Fort on the Arkansas River, and Fort St. Vrain and Fort Lupton on the Platte River are well known early trading posts.

John D. "Colonel Jack" Henderson built a trading post, known as Henderson Island, in 1859. It was on the South Platte River near where the town of Henderson is today. He did a booming business with the gold seekers headed for the foothills. He soon expanded into the freighting business to supply his trading post with the rapidly selling goods it needed. Henderson's many mules and oxen were turned loose to graze when not in use. One winter many of them had wandered too far and he had to go looking for them in the spring. When he found them, many miles away, they were in good shape and very fat. He had discovered the value of open range grazing in eastern Colorado, and soon expanded into the ranching business. Henderson may have been the first to use the name Deer Trail for the spot on the East Bijou where he found his livestock.

Henderson undoubtedly faced many Indian troubles during his years on the Colorado frontier. He eventually made enough money in the ranching business that he moved east to spend the rest of his life in peace. Ironically, many years later, on a trip to Colorado to visit some of his gold mines, he and eighteen others were slaughtered by Osage Indians before ever reaching Colorado.

During the 1860s the problems between the Indians and white settlers reached their peak in eastern Colorado. Wagon trains were attacked, horses and livestock stolen, settlers killed and women and children taken captive. Frontier forts, manned by U.S. Cavalry, were established for protection. These outposts were usually great distances apart, and communication was slow, so they were more reactive than preventative when Indian troubles arose.

The forts in eastern Colorado were mainly along the South Platte River to the north, along the Arkansas River to the south, in the foothills west of Denver, and in western Kansas. This left a vast area of Colorado's central plains with no protection.

Early military forts protecting eastern Colorado included; Fort Morgan, 1864-1868; Fort Collins, 1863-1867; Camp Weld, (then it was north of Denver, now 8th and Vallejo St.), 1861-1865; Fort Garland, (twenty-five miles south of Alamosa), 1858-1883; Rankin Camp, near Julesburg, est. 1864 (later changed to Fort Sedgwick); Fort Reynolds, (near Pueblo), 1867-1872; Fort Lyon, (on the Arkansas River near Las Animas), 1860-1897; and Fort Wallace, Kansas, (forty miles east of Cheyenne Wells, Colorado) 1865-1882.

As the population increased in this area, temporary Army camps were sometimes located where trouble was occurring. These camps were also used along the route of the Kansas Pacific Railroad during its construction, to protect the workers. In May 1870, Indians killed eleven railroad graders, wounded nineteen, and stole 400 head of stock near Kit Carson. Three companies of cavalry were sent from Fort Wallace, Kansas to help patrol the line, and all railroad workers were armed. There was a cavalry battalion under Colonel Reno stationed at River Bend during railroad construction in 1870. A more long term Army camp at Cedar Point was home to the Sixth cavalry at least through 1873.

Gregory and Susan Michno's book, "A Fate Worse Than Death", gives accounts of over a hundred women and children who were taken captive by Indians in the great plains area. Colorado stories include the 1864 capture of Anna Snyder who was taken near Booneville (between Pueblo and Fort Lyon). Her husband and the two other men in their party were all killed. Mrs. Snyder was beaten and abused so badly that she tore her dress into strips and hung herself from the tipi poles.

Sarah Morris and her two young sons, Joseph and Charlie were captured in 1865, when their ranch near Marino, Colorado, was attacked and all the men were killed. Sarah received eleven arrow wounds. Her youngest boy was killed, the other was taken from her and she never saw him again. Many years later, soldiers were able to negotiate a trade of two horses and some sugar for Sarah's release.

Clara Blinn and son Willie were traveling with an eight-wagon train in 1868, heading east from Fort Lyon, when they were attacked by Cheyenne. They held out for five days but in the end the men were killed, the wagons burned, and Clara and Willie carried off. They were traded and sold through several different tribes, including Black Kettle's, who also had two other white captives at that time. Clara and Willie were killed by their captors when the village where they were being held was attacked by George Custer's cavalry.

In 1868, Mrs. Henrietta Dietemann and her five year old son, John, were found dead near their homestead on Comanche Creek, five miles northeast of Kiowa. Mrs. Dietemann, her two children, her sister-in-law, and two hired hands were fleeing their home on foot, seeking safety in Middle Kiowa, after an Indian raid at their home. Henrietta had fallen a little behind the rest of the group, probably because she was seven months pregnant. Young John saw the Indians attack his mother. He pulled his hand free from the adults who were holding him and ran to her. Thirty Indians attacked the party who had gone to recover the bodies of the Dietemann family, but they were able to hold off the small band of Indians and escape with the bodies. The boy had been shot several times and his neck broken. Mrs. Dietemann had been shot, raped, stabbed, and scalped.

In November, 1864 the infamous Sand Creek Massacre took place on Big Sandy Creek northeast of Eads, about forty miles northeast of Fort Lyon. The Southern Cheyenne and Arapaho had been causing headaches for a couple of years prior to 1864. That spring, raids on roads and settlements had become so frequent it had virtually stopped traffic on the Santa Fe Trail. This was causing nervousness and inconvenience in Denver. Supplies couldn't get through and it was not considered safe for a party of less than one hundred to leave Denver.

Adding to this frenzy, in June of 1864, the Hungate family were working on a ranch near present day Elizabeth. They were brutally killed by Cheyenne and Arapaho Indians and the ranch burned to the ground. The mutilated bodies of Nathan and Ellen Hungate, their two year old and five month old daughters were brought to Denver and displayed before burial.

Citizens were panic stricken. They feared an Indian uprising like Minnesota suffered in 1862 when the Sioux wiped out entire white settlements in a revolt against the government's failed treaties and promises.

Governor Evans asked for help from Colonel Chivington who planned to wipe out all Indians on the eastern plains. After seeing the Hungate family, it didn't take long for Chivington to raise a volunteer army of several hundred men.

Unfortunately, Black Kettle's band of Cheyenne who received the retaliation at Sand Creek, were virtually wiped out. They were probably not the perpetrators. Black Kettle and six other Chiefs had met at Camp Weld to talk peace with Governor Evans in September of 1864. Sand Creek angered the Indians and caused many more years of raids and wars by the plains Indians.

In 1868, one of the well known later battles in eastern Colorado was Beecher's Island. It took place near Wray on the Arikaree River. Fifty Army scouts had been sent on patrol from Fort Wallace, Kansas, to check out reports they had received of Indian raids in that region. The scouts were attacked by two hundred or more Cheyenne. Although it offered no protection, they took shelter on a sand bar in the creek bed. The troops killed their horses and dug in behind them. The battle went on for nine days. On the second day, two men volunteered to try to escape and go to Fort Wallace for help. The two volunteers crawled on hands and knees through the grass and traveled at night on foot to finally reach Fort Wallace, seventy miles away. Six soldiers were killed and fifteen wounded by the time help arrived. Cheyenne Chief Roman Nose was killed at this battle, along with many other Cheyenne. The troops who came from Fort Wallace reported that, when they arrived, the smell from all the dead horses and men was unbearable.

The following year, 1869, another battle took place at Summit Springs, which is south of Sterling, between Akron and Atwood. A small band of Cheyenne Dog Soldiers had been raiding in north central Kansas and had taken women captives. A company of cavalry, along with fifty Pawnee scouts were sent after them. A fierce battle broke out when the Pawnee scouts, who were traveling ahead of the soldiers, encountered the Cheyenne camp. By the time the Cavalry got there most of the Cheyenne were dead or captured. A few had escaped. The Cheyenne did have two white women captives. They were killed by their captors, so the army would not have the satisfaction of rescuing them. However, one captive, Maria Weichel, shot twice in the chest, recovered.

Many of these later Indian battles and raids were the work of Cheyenne Dog Soldiers, which was a term used for young warriors who wanted to destroy all white settlers and had no interest in talking peace. Dog soldiers got their name because of their strange practice of selecting one warrior to take a stand at the forefront of a battle, pinned down like a dog. The warrior secured himself with a dog rope. This was a buffalo hide sash with one end around the warrior's shoulder and the other staked to the ground by a picket pin. Held there with no way to escape, he held off the attackers so the rest of the warriors could secure positions for the battle.

In the Medicine Lodge Treaty of 1867, the Cheyenne and Arapaho had agreed to leave eastern Colorado and go to reservations in Kansas and Oklahoma. However, it took many years for this to happen. The Utes, who were a little more peaceful tribe, were not sent to their reservation in Southwestern Colorado until 1880.

In June 1873, some Ute Indians were killed in Laramie, Wyoming. No one seemed to know why or by whom. The Utes on the eastern plains and in southern Colorado were threatening to make trouble over their tribesmen being killed. Governor Elbert asked a group of Utes, who were camped close to Denver, to come in and meet with him. He planned to ask them to remain calm until he could get to the bottom of what happened in Wyoming and see that those at fault were punished. The chief of this band of Utes was named Piah. He was not with the group that met with the governor. He was hunting buffalo somewhere on the plains. When the governor asked how he could talk to Piah, he was told, "You could send Piah a message. He gets his mail at Deer Trail." It may have seemed unusual to be communicating with the chief of the Utes by mail when most tribes were still communicating with smoke signals, but even stranger was the fact that Deer Trail did not have an official U.S. post office until 1875. Evidently they had their own mail and message system long before that.

Before Piah received his message to meet with the governor, there was trouble on the plains. Mr. A. K. Clarke, agent of the Kansas Pacific Railroad at Deer Trail sent the following telegram: "Deer Trail, Colorado, July 9, 1873 – To U.M. Curtis, Indian Interpreter at Denver: A band of eighteen Utes returned from the Little Republican this morning. They had a fight with a party of Arapaho and Cheyenne. Piah, Acupass and Colorado's Papoose had their ponies shot. Handthrope received a bullet on the metal on his breast, but the bullet did not go through it. The Utes killed four Arapahoes and secured the scalp of one. The Utes were camped on the Republican the next night after passing here, and the next morning the Arapahoes came upon them, but they killed no Utes. The Utes killed and captured twenty-four ponies. Thompson (The Indian agent) asked me to telegraph you this." This Rocky Mountain News article also gives the following description of Chief Piah: "Piah is a festive gentleman of the Ute persuasion, who sports good clothes in town, is saucy, speaks some English, and knows a thing or two."

Piah, Chief of the Utes

A. K. Clark, the depot agent at Deer Trail, who came to Colorado in 1868, later wrote a series of stories of his early experiences. In an 1873 story, he tells about Piah and his band of Indians coming and taking up residence on Clark's small ranch on Bijou Creek near Deer Trail. After the Indians and their large herd of horses had been camped there long enough to be using up all of his grass, Clark asked Piah to move to a new camp. Piah said, "This is old Indian camp, you move." Clark told him he would write to Indian agent Thompson if they did not move. Piah again refused and Clark wrote his letter. He received a reply from Thompson that said, "Tell Piah I say to move." Clark told this to Piah and he replied, "Alright Ute go."

1873 seemed to have been a significant year for Indian raids in eastern Colorado. In September of that year, two to three hundred Cheyenne Indians left the reservation in Fort Sill, Oklahoma, and seven hundred miles later entered southeastern Colorado. The military authorities at Fort Lyon, near Las Animas, ordered them to return to their reservation. They promised to do so and left, headed in that direction. However, they turned back and circled wide of Fort Lyon, half the band traveling south of the Arkansas River and half north of the river. The northern band headed north through the sparsely settled area between Sand Creek and Horse Creek, stealing horses and killing many more cattle than what they ate, along the way.

The first contact with settlers was at the Dowling ranch on October 2. They ransacked the house and took all the food as well as clothing, a gold watch, and money, and destroyed most everything else. The next day they appeared at Nash's sheep ranch. Chief Spotted Horse was with this band. He spoke good English, and he made himself at home in the house and conversed with Mr. Nash while his warriors killed sheep and stole horses outside. Spotted Horse took a gun from the house and left a sore-footed pony in exchange for it. Mr. Nash was just thankful that he, his two sons, and a hired man had been spared.

October 4, the Indians came to Liptrap's ranch, on Big Sandy, seventeen miles southwest of River Bend. The Liptraps were an older couple. Spotted Horse showed them his certificates from Fort Sill stating that he was a "good Indian," then commanded Mrs. Liptrap to cook food for them, which she did. As fast as one band was fed, another would come. The poor woman was kept at work all day until the last of the provisions were used up. The Indians left at dark and the Liptraps took what few belongings they had left and reached the English place, (their nearest neighbors), at dawn.

The Indians came next to the Hittson Ranch, which was on the north side of the Big Sandy about two miles northeast of Liptraps. They stole fifteen head of horses, provisions and a few articles from the house. As soon as the Indians were gone, the ranch foreman and two ranch hands rode to River Bend and telegraphed John Hittson, who was in Denver at the time. The telegram reported what they knew of the Indian raids thus far, and said the Indians were headed north and would probably reach Bijou Basin or Deer Trail in a couple of days.

John Hittson began rallying other ranchers and interested parties. He soon left Denver on a special train, furnished by the Kansas Pacific Railroad, with sixty-five men. Guns and ammunition had been issued by order of the governor. Because of not knowing the exact location of the Indians, five men were put off at Farmer's place on West Bijou (near Byers), fifteen at Hittson's ranch at Deer Trail, and forty-five went on to River Bend. Each of the groups would gather more men and head in the direction where they thought the Indians had gone, they planned to come at them from the north, south, and east.

W.H.H. Cramner led the group leaving from River Bend, which numbered about forty-five. Before going too far, they came to a camp site which the Indians had just left that morning. By the camp, they could tell that the Indian's number was larger than any estimates they had heard so far, possibly three hundred or more. The trail leading from the camp showed that the Indians were traveling in staggered columns, five or ten miles wide, covering the whole country, to kill game and take in all the ranches in their path.

When Cramner's force reached the English place they found the Liptraps and Moores there. All three families were packing and preparing to leave. They said a small band of Indians had circled the house all day. The men had held them off with guns. As they finally rode away one brave came close enough to yell "Heap Cheyenne come," just before he left. Cramner was hesitant to pursue the Cheyenne with his small force. Fortunately, before they left English's they were joined by about twenty men who came from Rocky Ford in pursuit of the Indians. Then shortly, John Hittson reached that point with thirty-two men.

As they rode toward Bijou Basin, (which is about twenty miles southwest of Deer Trail) they had ten men riding ahead to scout. The scouts came across four Indians with a pack mule. Several shots were exchanged in an attempt to recapture the mule. With the sound of the shots, Indian pickets began appearing on every high ridge within sight. This was a bit unnerving to the white forces, but when the Indians saw the larger number of their pursuers, they began leaving with greater speed.

By evening, Hittson's forces were convinced they were too far behind the Indians. They made camp for the night. When they resumed their pursuit the next morning, they came upon a campsite that the Indians had apparently left in a hurry. Only a few small fires had been started, cooking utensils, knives, etc. had been left behind. Evidently they had come closer to overtaking them the night before than they thought. It also appeared that the Indians, at this point, had turned south toward Fort Lyon. The cowboy army paralleled the retreating Indians until troops from the Sixth Cavalry at River Bend and Fort Lyon and Cavalry from

Fort Wallace, Kansas were dispatched to escort them out of the state and back to Fort Sill.

It was later reported that the Cheyenne who had gone south of the Arkansas River to do their raiding had killed a ranchman named Ward, on Butte Creek, southwest of Fort Lyon. He had tried to resist when they began killing his cattle, and they killed him and burned his home.

The last known Indian trouble in eastern Colorado occurred in 1878 near Cheyenne Wells. Joe McLane was apparently killed by a small band of Ute Indians. Joe started toward Cheyenne Wells from his ranch on the morning of July 30, and was never seen or heard from again. The next day Joe's mare, with a colt following, came in from the north and was caught by a station foreman. There was blood on the seat of the saddle, on the coat tied behind, on the pommel, and the mane. The Utes had been in Cheyenne Wells a few days before, wanting food, tobacco, etc. which was given to them. They rode out in the direction of Old Cheyenne Wells, a former stage station on the Smokey Hill Trail.

Lewis, Joe's brother rode immediately to Old Cheyenne Wells. There on the ridge he saw a band of Indians. He rode to the track and flagged a train and telegraphed the post to have a party sent to help with the search. He rode on to the ranch and assembled his own search party.

It was easy following the trail left by Joe's mare because of the colt following. They came to a ravine about twelve miles from the station, where his mare jumped and then doubled back on her tracks. Indian pony tracks crossed and re-crossed in all directions. The tracks went up a steep bank and something fell and left an impression in the soft clay. Moccasin tracks were very plain in this area. The searchers saw Indians on a ridge to the north, and then scouting parties to their rear. As there was only five in Lewis' search party, it would have been folly to attack them. They returned to get more men.

11

The circumstances were telegraphed to Fort Wallace. Later when a squad was sent from the fort, they camped for dinner about five miles north of Arapahoe station, rode to Cheyenne Wells, camped all night and returned to the post the following morning.

In the meantime parties of about fifty had organized up the road at Carson, Hugo, River Bend and Deer Trail. They received word that the Indians were camped around Cedar Point, so they headed in that direction. There were no Indians at Cedar Point.

Lewis McLane spent all his free time for three years riding the plains looking for his brother Joe. Joe's skeleton was finally found March 31, 1881, twenty miles northwest of Cheyenne Wells and positively identified.

Resources: Rocky Mountain News - June 14, 1867, Aug. 27, 1868, July 9, 1873, July 10, 1873, Oct. 4, 1873, Oct. 11, 1873; Denver Daily Times - Oct. 9, 1873; Denver Daily Tribune - Aug. 4, 1878, Aug. 21, 1878; Colorado Springs Gazette - Oct. 4, 1873; Colorado Magazine - Colorado Historical Society; Field and Farm Magazine - Denver Public Library; "A Fate Worse than Death," Gregory & Susan Michno; "The First Five Years of The Railroad Era in Colorado," E.O. Davis; "A Wild West History of Frontier Colorado," Jolie Anderson Gallagher.

JOHN NATHAN HITTSON

A True Pioneer

John Hittson, also known as 'Cattle Jack', and the 'Cattle King of the Texas and Colorado Frontier', definitely had a big part in settling the West. He was in on the ground floor of the Texas cattle drives, commencing the same year as Loving and Goodnight. It is said that he trailed more cattle to Colorado between 1868 and 1876 than Chisum, Loving, Goodnight and all the other 'long drivers', as they were called.

Hittson moved his headquarters to Deer Trail in 1872, purchasing a ranch from James E. Patterson. Hittson and Patterson had been partners on bringing Texas cattle to Patterson's Deer Trail ranch since 1866, making them, if not the first, among the very first settlers around Deer Trail. Patterson's ranch was on the west side of Middle Bijou Creek, about 3 miles northwest of Deer Trail. Undoubtedly this site was chosen because of the six springs flowing from the hillside. Their original plan was to hold the cattle on the Deer Trail ranch for sale to the miners in Denver and the foothills. Soon Hittson recognized the potential of open range grazing year around in the area.

Hittson was no stranger to frontier troubles such as Indians, Comancheros, cattle rustling, and gun play. The legacy probably began with John's father Jesse Hittson. In 1820, Jesse and a party of trappers were captured by Indians on the Kentucky frontier. They were tied to stakes and were doomed. Miraculously, one of the men worked his hands free and they all escaped.

Jesse later moved his family to Tennessee where John Nathan was born in 1831. After the family was raised, in 1855, three Hittson families left Tennessee headed for the Texas frontier. Twenty-four year old John, his eighteen year old wife Selena, John's younger brother William and wife Martha, their father Jesse and mother Mary Ann, settled west of Fort Worth in Palo Pinto County. This was about the farthest west any white settlers had tried to ranch at that time, barely east of what was considered Indian country.

In 1857, John was elected as the first sheriff of Palo Pinto County. In 1860, Sheriff Hittson and the few other settlers in Palo Pinto were again reminded of the dangers of the area in which they lived. A raiding party of Kiowas and Comanches killed and scalped a farmer named John Brown in his field and helped themselves to all his livestock. They moved on to the Thompson place and stole seven horses, then headed for the Sherman place.

The Sherman family was just sitting down to dinner when the Indians burst in. They froze in their seats. A warrior grabbed Mr. Sherman by his hair and jerked him out of his chair. Soon other Indians did the same to the rest of the family. The Indians then sat down and began eating hungrily, ignoring the family, who quickly headed outside and down the road. Unfortunately, as soon as the raiding party had demolished the meal and the house, they rode after the family. Mr. Sherman was able to hide the children in the bushes, but they pulled Mrs. Sherman onto a horse and rode away. She was later found not far away. She had been molested, scalped and badly wounded, she lived for only four days. Around her lay the ripped up pages of the family Bible, which the Indians had stolen from the house.

The citizens sent a letter to the governor reporting that the Indians had violated both white womanhood and the Christian Holy Book, and demanded he commission a civilian militia to apprehend them. A hundred men were soon gathered and the expedition began. John and William Hittson were in the force. For two weeks they combed the countryside, until they finally spotted a group of Indians in the distance. Soon the chase was on, Indians scattered in all directions. After the militia regrouped, most of the Indians had escaped, a few were killed, mostly squaws. They had captured a young boy and one squaw with a baby.

After they got a better look at the squaw, they discovered that she had blue eyes. Someone remarked about the old legend of Cynthia Ann Parker, who had been stolen by Indians in 1836 when she was nine years old, and though many had tried, she had never been found. The squaw spoke up and said, "Me Cynthia Ann." She was taken to her Uncle Isaac Parker, who had offered a reward and searched for her for nearly twenty-five years. It was said that she was never truly happy and missed her Indian husband and the two sons she left behind. One of these sons was Quanah Parker, who became a fierce warrior and plagued white settlers for many years. Years later, in 1868, John Hittson was also a member of a militia group who rode in pursuit of Quanah Parker and his band, after they stole 1500 head of cattle from a Texas rancher named Murphy.

Cynthia Ann's Indian husband, Peta Nokona, heard Cynthia had been taken to Palo Pinto. He was not aware that she had long ago been taken on to her Uncle's home in Tarrant County. Peta Nokona raided continuously in that area until his death a few years later. Many families in the area, including the Hittson families, moved to "Camp Cooper," a nearby abandoned army camp. It afforded them some protection and safety in numbers, they lived there for nearly two years.

John gave up his job as sheriff a few years later when he found himself, and the law, were helpless against the strong vigilante movement known as the O.L.M. 'Old Law Mob', which had been at work in west Texas for many years out of necessity. They were better equipped than he was to handle Indian raids, which was the most common "lawlessness" at that time anyway. John did not approve of their methods, but was powerless to stop them.

John then began branding wild cattle and ranching with his family. In 1864, Hittson partnered with other ranchers and trailed a herd of cattle to Mexico. It was a big risk. They would have to travel an unknown route, crossing through Indian country, and there was the dangerous crossing of the Rio Grande River. Also, the Civil War was in progress so they had to avoid any armies because trade with Mexico had been outlawed by the Confederacy. They were able to overcome all those dangers and made it to Mexico with their herd where they received ten to eighteen dollars per head in silver Pesos. They then faced their greatest dilemma when they were confronted and interrogated by angry Mexicans, who were not willing to let them go back across the border with the Mexican silver. However, they finally won that argument and were permitted to return to Texas. On the south bank of the river they saw the bodies of three Texas intruders whom the same Mexican vigilantes had just killed.

When they arrived home, Hittson discovered all the buildings at his homestead had been burned and his family was gone. In a panic, they immediately rode to nearby Fort Davis. To his relief, Selena and the children had escaped to the fort. The surrounding ranchers had gathered all the families and taken them to the fort when they were warned of a raiding party headed their way.

In 1865, while the Hittson brothers were hunting wild cattle for another drive, their party, (consisting of John and William and John's eleven year old son Jesse and two other cowboys, Freeman Ward, and Press McCarty) were attacked by Comanches. Immediately John grabbed Jesse and pulled him onto his horse with him. In that small lapse of time, John was hit by an arrow that pierced his leg and clear through the leather of his saddle into the horse. Freeman Ward, who had stopped to retrieve his new coonskin hat, made for him by Mrs. Hittson, was killed. Press McCarty escaped and rode for nearby Camp Cooper. John, William, and Jesse took shelter under a rock bluff that offered some protection. John's horse had been hit by more than a few arrows and was in serious condition. William killed the horse at the mouth of the cavern, forming a small barricade. Indian ponies could be heard on the bluff above them. Soon rocks and boulders were raining down on the mouth of their shelter. Their only musket was put out of commission by one of these falling rocks, leaving them with one Colt pistol with only two rounds left. The assault of arrows continued, both John and William were hit a second time. Soon the rocks that had been pushed down upon them formed a barrier for their protection. They used their last shot about dark, and by this time it was apparent that no help was coming from Camp Cooper. About midnight, the three struck out. William was scouting in the lead, and Jesse led a seriously injured John on their one remaining horse. When they got to Camp Cooper they found out that Press McCarty had made it to the camp safely, but had reported that everyone else in the party had been killed. The bluff where they survived the Indian attack is known as Hittson's Bluff to this day.

Both Hittson bothers recovered from their wounds, but their intended 1865 cattle drive to Mexico did not happen. By the time they had a herd gathered in the spring of 1866, things had changed. The Mexican market had dried up, but James Patterson, a beef contractor at Fort Sumner, New Mexico Territory, who had traveled the Pecos Trail in 1865, came to Texas seeking a dependable supply of cattle, not only for U.S. Army contracts and to feed the nine thousand Navajo and Apache on a reservation at Fort Sumner, New Mexico, but also for a growing Colorado market.

The Pecos Trail was 1,000 miles of treachery, but that was nothing new to these Texas cow drivers. Amazingly, the trail headed southwest from Palo Pinto until it reached the Pecos River just south of New Mexico's southern border, then basically followed the Pecos river north through New Mexico, then continuing almost straight north into Colorado. As dangerous as this route was, it was deemed much safer than travel anywhere through the west Texas Indian country.

Because of John Hittson's late start due to his injuries, Oliver Loving and Charles Goodnight beat him to the trail by two weeks. Hittson's herd was joined by a wagon train of eight wagons led by

17

Thomas Stockton. Both parties were seeking safety in numbers for the dangerous trip. Included in the wagon train was John Selman. Years later, in 1895, John Selman killed John Wesley Harden in an El Paso saloon.

Second place on this trip might not have been such a bad idea. Hittson's crew often saw signs of unshod ponies following the Loving herd. They met a young drover that Loving had sent back to camp to have an arrow wound treated. They also saw signs of the trouble Loving had at 'Horsehead Crossing.'

Horsehead Crossing was the point where the trail reached the Pecos River. It was preceded by ninety miles of waterless Texas desert, the most treacherous part of the trail. Hittson decided to push both men and beast to the limit by traveling day and night in an attempt to reach water as soon as possible. They stopped for an hour's rest each day, and crossed the ninety mile stretch in three days. As they neared the crossing, they found dead cattle scattered along the trail. The banks of the Pecos were lined with dead cattle. The river was dammed up in places by the bodies of dead cattle. Loving's cattle had caught a whiff of the water long before they reached the river and stampeded. Nearly dying of thirst, they all plunged into the river at once and many were trampled under and drown in the commotion.

Hittson chose to drive clear of Horsehead crossing and stayed on the north side of the river almost into New Mexico. Hittson sold his herd at Fort Sumner, except for 100 head which he contracted with James Patterson to trail them to Patterson's ranch at Deer Trail. As they left New Mexico, they followed a new trail, traveled by Patterson the previous year. It went slightly east of the old route through Raton Pass and entered Colorado just east of Trinidad. This was made necessary by an old settler named Wooten, who had camped at Raton Pass and was charging 10 cents per head for driving cattle through the Pass. There is a town east of Trinidad on the Purgatoire River named Patterson's Crossing. The Pecos trail and this new route into Colorado would later become known as the Goodnight-Loving trail.

The wagon train had halted at Fort Union, between Fort Sumner and the Colorado border. Thomas Stockton built a hotel there, which became the famous Clifton House, an important stop for the stage coming from Colorado.

On the return trip to Texas, Hittson had sold most of the horses. The six men who were returning with him, were riding in one wagon pulled by oxen. John and William rode along beside. Even before leaving New Mexico they began seeing signs of Indian trouble. Above Pecos Falls, they saw a white man's head stuck on a pole. They could see distant smoke signals for much of the way. As they completed the ninety mile dry crossing and neared the Concho River, they were attacked by a band of thirty Kiowas. The men all dismounted and abandoned the wagon to take shelter in the trees along the river bank and prepared to fight. They were relieved, when after a short time, the Indians ceased their attack. Their relief was short lived when they discovered the reason the Indians quit the fight was that they were leaving the scene with the Hittson wagon and supplies, and all their oxen and horses.

They were eighty miles from home, but the men had no choice but to walk. They traveled at night, not knowing if the Indians would return to finish them off at any time. They dug into snow banks and huddled together in the daytime. They shot a jack rabbit when they could, but were very careful with their precious ammunition. All their spare ammunition had gone with the wagon. Four days before Christmas, hungry and nearly frozen, the men limped into their little community at Fort Davis.

John Hittson continued gathering cattle in Texas and driving them to Colorado every year. He, and his family, and his drovers had many more scrapes with the Indians. A decade later a rancher reported finding an old brindle steer with Hittson's brand on its side. On the other side was branded, "7-4-68 INDIANS HOT AS HELL JH"

John Hittson 1831-1880

During this time the reputation of "Cattle Jack" was growing to mythical proportions. By 1871, newspapers all across the nation were telling of John Hittson's adventures on the frontier. One of the stories written about in a Denver newspaper in 1871 was, "Cattle Jack trail boss, wearing two Navy Colt pistols and carrying an 1866 rimfire, .44 caliber Winchester 'Yellow Boy', leading 1,000 or more wild Texas Longhorns down Larimer Street in Denver, backed up by his outfit of bearded heavily armed men." This description of Hittson also supports his formidable appearance, "over six feet tall, long red hair and a beard, weighing two hundred and twenty-five pounds."

Also in 1871, Hittson began formulating a plan to go into New Mexico and round up cattle that had been stolen from Texas cattlemen by Indians, Mexicans, and Comancheros, by his estimation 100,000 head or more. He acquired power of attorney from about two hundred ranchers giving him authority to seize any cattle with their brands not accompanied by a bill of sale. He then began seeking gunmen for the trip.

Cattle buyer James Patterson sold his "Six Springs" ranch at Deer Trail to John Hittson July 11, 1872. By this time all parts of the plan had come together. Patterson and Hittson and about sixty men departed from Deer Trail and met Stockton, who had another dozen men at Clifton House in New Mexico. With the backing of the governor of Texas, and the cooperation of the Army, the three groups spread out and canvased the New Mexico territory for stolen cattle. Hittson stressed using peaceful means, if possible, when recovering the cattle. They had only a couple minor shooting incidents in which two New Mexico men were killed when they fired on the Texas cowboys. It was claimed that they had gathered eighteen thousand head of cattle during this six week raid.

John returned to his Deer Trail ranch and began building his empire, presumably bringing along many of the recovered New Mexico cattle. A few years later when Hittson paid his tax of $3 per head, his bill was $300,000. He constructed a large southern style white frame house, and his wife and family soon joined him there. There was a separate kitchen, a large root cellar and spring house, and many other outbuildings including a barn that still stands in 2014.

Hittson ranch house, Deer Trail, Colorado,
built in 1872. It was destroyed by fire in 1923

21

Cattle Jack's presence and influence at Deer Trail elevated it to the major shipping point in northern Colorado on the Kansas Pacific Railroad. This status was boosted when Denver outlawed driving cattle within three miles of the city. In 1874, many Denver dignitaries came out by train to celebrate the doubling in size of the Deer Trail stockyards and the installation of new Fairbanks scales. Afterward, Hittson invited everyone to his ranch for an elaborate party in honor of the occasion.

In September 1873, three hundred Cheyenne, who had left the reservation in Oklahoma, passed through the country headed for Montana. Hittson received word from his foreman south of Hugo that the Indians were raiding ranches and butchering cattle. Hittson notified Colorado's Territorial Governor Elbert. Recognizing Hittson's reputation as an Indian fighter, the governor sent supplies and ammunition to Deer Trail on a 'special' Kansas Pacific train. The next day Hittson led thirty-two armed men out of Deer Trail in pursuit of the Indians.

The cowboy army caught up with the Cheyenne on October 6. They paralleled the movements of the large band of Indians, estimated at over two hundred. Finally Chief Spotted Tail and two warriors rode to the head of Hittson's column and confronted him. Cattle Jack asked, "Why are you robbing houses, killing cattle, and taking horses?" After a long silence, Spotted Tail responded, "We are no horse thieves" and rode away. Hittson's men kept up the escort for two more days until the Cavalry arrived and took over the escort.

Things seemed to start going bad for Hittson in 1875. Maybe, like many others of his day, he had just out lived his era. Most of the Indians were staying on reservations now. Texas rangers and other lawmen were eliminating the need for vigilantes and gun fights to settle disputes. Even the 'long drive' cattle drives were growing fewer. Due to railroad expansion in the west, cattle markets were becoming more accessible.

There were rumors that Hittson faced multiple lawsuits alleging that he sold more than his share of the cattle recovered from New Mexico. The truth was that the sale of all the recovered cattle would barely have covered the expenses for the mission. In April 1875, the Colorado Supreme Court awarded over three thousand dollars in a finding against Hittson, cause unknown. He began selling off cattle, possibly to pay other judgments.

Apparently John's troubles got to him. He began drinking more than usual. He became very disagreeable when drinking. On one such spree, for unknown reasons, John got in a shootout with J. M. Maxwell on a street in Deer Trail. John got in the first blast with a shotgun. Maxwell returned fire with his revolver. Hittson escaped harm but Maxwell received a couple of buckshot wounds in his left hand. Unfortunately, a stray bullet struck a local Deer Trail boy named Brown in the foot. The district court in Denver blamed Hittson for the episode and he was held on a bond of four thousand dollars. Hittson, it seems, also blamed himself for the violence. Bad blood remained between Hittson and Maxwell for many years. There was an incident in 1879 when Maxwell threatened to kill Hittson at a local saloon. The bar owner managed to keep the two apart, possibly saving someone's life.

In 1877, when Hittson was temporarily 'on the wagon', he accidently shot himself while playing ten pins at a Deer Trail saloon. Apparently some gesture with his arm caused him to hit the gun in his pocket. When the gun hit the floor it discharged hitting Hittson in the leg. A doctor was sent for and came out from Denver on a special train to treat the wound. Hittson declared that he had never shot himself when he was drinking, thus ended the dry spell.

In 1878, his son Jesse, who had been ranching with his father since they came to Colorado, sold out all his share and left to establish a ranch in the Texas panhandle, possibly due to a rift between them. Jesse later hired Pat Garrett, who would shoot Billy the Kid a few years later, to be his foreman on his Texas ranch.

By 1879, things couldn't get much worse. Hittson was indicted for robbery in Las Vegas, New Mexico. No information is known if anything ever came of those charges. Also that year, the Rocky Mountain News reported that Hittson "got into a difficulty with some party and attempted to shoot him. The fellow turned on and assaulted Hittson." Afterwards Hittson was seen in Denver with a badly bruised face.

Also in 1879, Hittson sold almost all his remaining cattle to his son-in-law John Hayes. Probably due partly to his financial and legal problems, and also to the hard winters experienced in the preceding years. By 1880, Hittson had to purchase a railroad car load of feed to keep his cattle from starving.

On Christmas day 1880, John Nathan Hittson, aged 49, was killed when the front wheel came off the carriage he was driving as he crossed the railroad track between his ranch and Deer Trail. Two of his men found his body as they returned home from picking up feed at the Deer Trail railroad depot. Farther along, they found the wagon with the wheel missing and a very excitable team. The harness was badly twisted as if the carriage had rolled several times, probably as the frightened team ran away after the accident.

News of Hittson's death appeared in newspapers in New York, Chicago, Kansas, Colorado, and Texas. He was laid to rest in the new Riverside Cemetery in Denver. Five years later no one from the family remained in Deer Trail. Hittson's sons-in-law, Fine Ernest and W.H.H. Cramner, who were also prominent ranchers in the Deer Trail, Agate, and River Bend area, had moved to Denver. Mrs. Hittson took the younger children and returned to Mineral Wells in Palo Pinto County, Texas. Jesse Hittson sold his Texas holdings and returned to Colorado, for a short time, to manage his father's estate. For a few years he also ran the Arapaho Land and Cattle Company with a range on the Bijou and Big Beaver Creeks. Jesse leased, and later sold, Hittson's Six Springs ranch to C. B. Rhodes who named it the White Ranch because of Hittson's large white house. Unfortunately, the house burned to the ground in 1923. All that remains in 2014 is a barn and a few foundations.

Many years after his death, John Hittson's estate received numerous small "Indian depredation claims" from the government. In typical government fashion, the largest claim for $15,000 was paid to Hittson's estate in 1909. It was to cover his losses of cattle and horses in Texas in 1870.

Resources: "John Hittson, Cattle King On The Texas and Colorado Frontier", by Vernon Maddux; "The Life and Times of "Cattle Jack" John Nathan Hittson", Kansas Cowboy, 2004; Denver Post – Oct. 28, 1898; Congressional records; Rocky Mountain News, various issues.

CATTLE GULCH

And The Texas Cattle War

After gold was discovered in the Colorado Rockies in 1859, prospectors, miners, and gold seekers of every kind began streaming into Colorado to make their fortunes. Colorado was a sparsely settled wilderness at that time, but it grew overnight, and became a Territory in 1861. This population boom soon opened up a market for Texas beef. Although there were ranchers in Colorado, their small herds could not supply the huge demand for beef.

Following the Civil war in 1865, there were five million wild longhorn cattle roaming free in Texas. Soldiers returning from the war, and other settlers, began gathering these wild cattle and accumulating large herds. However, they were sold only for hides and horns from $1 to $3 per head in Texas because they were so plentiful. These Texas entrepreneurs began driving their cattle north to various railheads and markets to get higher prices. The first herds began coming into Colorado in 1866 where they sold for $30 to $40 per head to supply the miners. The route they used was known as the Pecos Trail, and later as the Loving Goodnight Trail. It followed the Pecos River up through New Mexico and entered Colorado near Trinidad.

There soon developed a problem when native cattle of Colorado and other northern states, known as American cattle, began dying after coming in contact with the Texas longhorn cattle. This was caused by the disease which became known as 'Texas cattle fever'. Its causes and origins were not understood at that time, but it was caused by a tick carried by the longhorn cattle. These southern cattle had roamed wild for so long that they were tough as a boot and virtually immune to every disease, so while they were unaffected by the tick, all American cattle they came in contact with would contract the disease, which was always fatal. Many northern herds were being wiped out completely.

By 1868, many states including Colorado, had followed Chicago's huge cattle market's lead and banned Texas cattle from entering the state. This act was not only, understandably unpopular with Texas cattlemen, it was also opposed by miners, merchants, and other businessmen in Colorado because the beef was needed to supply the great demand. Because of this controversy and the general lack of law enforcement at the time, Texas cattle continued to be driven into Colorado and other states. Colorado ranchers formed an association in 1868 with the explicit purpose of keeping out the Texas beeves but found they had little political support to stop them.

In April 1869, two Texas drovers named John Dawson and Joel Curtis had camped, with their herd of two thousand longhorns, in Douglas County, Colorado. This location would be part of Elbert County when it was split from Douglas in 1874. Both men had driven cattle to Colorado in the past in such company as Charles Goodnight, Oliver Loving, Tom Stockton, Clay Allison, and others. In the middle of the night they were awakened by earth shattering gunfire. Before the men were armed and mounted, the herd was stampeded across the countryside. Many cattle were killed or injured in the attack. The Texans thought they had been attacked by Indians.

The next morning, the area where the cattle had been bedded down the previous night was littered with dead or injured cattle. When the count was made, it was less than fifty head, still a big loss. When the herders began trying to gather the scattered cattle, they asked around at some of the ranches if they had seen any of their lost cattle. The settlers confessed that they were the ones who had stampeded the herd, because there was a law against their diseased cattle being in Colorado and they wanted them to take them back where they belonged. The ranchers warned the Texans that next time they might not stop with shooting cows. The Texans were able to gather less than fifteen hundred head before they got nervous and decided to move on.

The camp site where this happened was named Cattle Gulch, because of all the cattle bones that remained there for many years. It is still known by that name today. It is located about six miles west of Agate just east of Wilson Creek.

Newspapers were critical of the men responsible for the raid, saying that even if the Texans were breaking the law the Colorado cattlemen had no right damaging other people's property. When charges were pressed and the case came to court, the Texas trail boss was fined fifty dollars and the owners of the herd were not even charged. Complaint was made against seventy-seven citizens of Douglas County (later Elbert County) charging them with stampeding and killing a lot of Texas cattle the property of Mr. Dawson and Mr. Curtis. Charges were heard by Judge Eyster and three citizens were held on $2,500 bond to appear in the next term of District Court. No names were given and the results of that case are unknown.

Some time after this incident, as Texas fever was becoming more understood, it was discovered, more or less by accident, that if a Texas herd spent a winter in either Colorado or the northern New Mexico mountains that the cold temperatures would kill the ticks which infested the cattle and they could then graze with any American stock with no danger of infection. There was such a large profit to be made that

Texas drivers could afford to plan their drives to include a few months stop before proceeding on north. Most herds were 'seasoned', as it was called, after that, but unfortunately not all. Therefore, the bad feelings toward Texas cattle continued for some time.

Resources: Colorado Transcript (Golden) June 23, 1869, July 21, 1869; Rocky Mountain News Dec. 4, 1868, April 12, 1869, April 16, 1869; A Wild West History of Frontier Colorado, Jolie Anderson Gallagher; Dawson, Goodnight and the Great American Cattle Drives, Gene Lamm

MAJOR G. W. GRAHAM

Hard to Kill, Hard to Keep.

A special dispatch from Hugo, Colorado, dated September 10, 1873, contained the following particulars of the attempted robbery of the United States paymaster at River Bend:

"A bold attempt was made at River Bend this morning, at day-break, to rob the United States paymaster, Major Brooks, as he was going from the train to the camp of the Sixth Cavalry, about three miles from River Bend, to pay off the troops. He got off the westbound passenger train and was met by Captain Irwin and Lieutenant Wetmore of the Sixth Cavalry, with an ambulance. Mrs. Roberts, wife of the post trader, was also in the ambulance. A short distance from the station they were halted by two men on foot, who were masked. Three shots were fired by them from a shotgun. One charge taking effect in Captain Irvin's back. At first his injuries were considered slight, but he has since commenced bleeding internally. Another shot was fired by the robbers from a pistol, the ball passing across Major Brooks' lap and through Mrs. Roberts' hand, making a painful wound. Lieutenant Wetmore then fired his pistol at one of the robbers, named G. W. Graham, formerly captain of the Tenth Cavalry at Fort Leavenworth. The ball passed through his body, just below the heart. He is dying. The other robber, John Dick, formerly keeper of No. 1 stage station on the Atchison, Topeka and Santa Fe railroad, escaped, but the cavalry are after him, with hopes of his capture."

The next day it was reported that Graham was still alive. Dick had not yet been captured. A squad of cavalry, under charge of W. H. H. Cramner, trailed him to a point west of Hugo, where the trail was lost. Captain Irwin's injuries were not as serious as first thought, and he recovered.

Major G. W. Graham was placed under arrest and taken by train to the county hospital at Denver to receive medical attention for his wound. Under this treatment his recovery was remarkably speedy. In less than two weeks he escaped from his sick room. Two days later he was re-captured on the streets of Denver and taken to the Larimer Street prison to await trial.

When his trial was held a month later, he was found guilty of "conspiracy against the government and an attempt to defraud the same by assaulting Major Brooks, an army paymaster, with the intent to rob him of United States funds." He was sentenced to two years in the penitentiary at Canon City, and the payment of one thousand dollars. He was committed at the penitentiary in December 1873.

George W. Graham was a native of New York. He entered the army in 1861 at the age of nineteen, and served until 1870. He was a perfect athlete, a splendid horseman, and an accurate shot. He was also a schemer, a con-artist, and a daring and unscrupulous man. During the Civil War he was a partisan commander of Union forces in North Carolina. Throughout the war he was credited with many heroic acts. He saved the life of Brigadier General Wessell at the risk of his own. He stopped the pursuit of the enemy army by setting fire to a bridge single handedly, under heavy fire, saving his entire company.

At the end of the War, he was a First Lieutenant and was assigned to duty in the West. He soon advanced to Major, and became a favorite at Fort Leavenworth, Kansas. While serving there, he met and became engaged to one of the most attractive ladies of Leavenworth. The night before the wedding was to take place, Major Graham was arrested and taken to jail to face a court-martial. The evidence before the court established the fact that Major Graham, while serving in the United States Army, had been the secret head of a band of horse thieves, and had systematically stolen and sold horses from the stables of the government.

The court-martial sentenced the Major to be dishonorably dismissed from the service, and to serve a term of ten years in a military prison. However, through some unknown influence or error, the only part of the sentence that was carried out was the dishonorable discharge. Major Graham left Kansas immediately for Denver, where if his larcenous ways continued, he did not get caught until his attempt at robbing the paymaster at River Bend.

It seems that two years was too long a time for Major Graham to stay behind bars. In May 1874, he instigated a plot to escape. One of the convicts somehow had come in possession of a key which would unlock the lower tier of cells. Major Graham made believe he was taken with violent pains in his stomach. He asked the guard to go to the cell above and get him some laudanum. The guard, seeing the extreme pain Graham was in, did so. When the guard returned, the prisoners had let themselves out of their cells and jumped the guard and locked him in one of the cells. They used their key to release a total of eight prisoners. They then helped themselves to food from the cook room and guns from the office.

In June 1874, Major Graham and three of the other escapees appeared in the mining town of Rosita, (about forty miles south of Canon City, near Westcliff). They told the town's people they were with a survey crew out to locate a stage line from Canon City through Rosita to San Juan. Graham invited the people to a meeting that evening to discuss the possibilities of Rosita's prosperous future. Everyone was very excited about this news and everyone attended the meeting, scarcely a citizen remained at home that night. While the town was so quiet, the four escapees helped themselves to food, clothes, boots, guns and various other necessities.

A posse rode out after the men the next day and discovered the convicts hiding in a cabin south of Rosita. Major Graham stepped out of the cabin, not suspecting there was a posse hidden in the nearby rocks. Several shots were fired at Graham, who fell face down to the ground and was presumed dead. One other prisoner was hit, the rest surrendered. A doctor was sent for, and after examining the men, determined neither would likely die. Graham, although being hit several times, received only one serious wound in the shoulder. The two men were taken to Rosita where they were cared-for for several weeks before being taken back to Canon City.

Graham was returned to the penitentiary in July 1874. However, he did not even serve out his original two year sentence, let alone any additional time for his escape, or the Rosita robbery. Instead he was discharged in August 1875, his record states, "according to act of congress." After being sentenced to a total of twelve years, Graham served only eighteen months.

Evidently, Major Graham enjoyed his recuperation period in Rosita, because following his release from the penitentiary he returned to Rosita where he opened a small whiskey den. It was probably there that he plotted and arranged, with others, the "jumping" of the Pocahontas mine. His men held the mine for several days. Graham, who was not even at the mine, got into a fight with a miner and shot him in the foot, then fled to the Pocahontas mine. By then a large group of miners were determined to storm the mine and take it back. As Graham approached the mine, his men yelled for him to turn around and run, but before he could, he was pierced by twenty-five bullets. From this scrape Major Graham did not escape, he died instantly.

October 30, 1875, about two o'clock, the funeral of Major George W. Graham passed through the dense crowd that lined Tyndall Street in Rosita. In a small open wagon, drawn by a mule team, was a five dollar coffin containing the body of Graham. The driver sat on the coffin. Behind the wagon walked one solitary pedestrian, a constable, who felt that having a corpse on his hands, it was his official duty to bury it. And thus was put under ground all that remained of this so talented, heroic, wicked and desperate man of the west.

Resources: Rocky Mountain News, Sept. 10, 1873; Pueblo Chieftain, Sept. 5, 1873, Sept. 12, 1873, Sept. 16, 1873, June 17, 1874, Oct. 15, 1875; Boulder Banner, Nov. 11, 1875; Las Animas Leader, Sept. 27, 1873, Nov. 29, 1873; Lake City Silver World, Oct. 30, 1875; Denver Mirror, Oct. 12, 1873; Denver Daily Times, May 28, 1874; Colorado State Penitentiary.

RIVER BEND DUEL

Not the First or the Last

*River Bend stage station on the Smokey Hill
Trail, prior to 1870. Sign says "Store – Saloon"*

River Bend, Colorado was a bustling frontier town in 1876. One fateful day in June, 1876, River Bend became the scene of a deadly old west gun fight, in which Alfred D. Jessup, Jr. was killed. This was undoubtedly not River Bend's first nor its last deadly battle, but probably one of the earliest that was recorded in the newspapers.

It is believed that River Bend was established around 1858. It was originally located on a big bend of Big Sandy Creek about six miles northwest of Limon. It began as a stage stop on the Smoky Hill Trail. It had a hotel, store, and a livery stable. The hotel probably contained an eating establishment and a saloon. It became the meeting place for the early cowboys and ranchers in the vast eastern Colorado open range, and a center of trade for settlers, travelers, and Indians. It had only six dwellings before the Kansas Pacific Railroad came through in 1870.

When the railroad was laying out its route, it wanted a more level area for its station near River Bend, so the depot, water tank, section houses, etc. were built about two miles to the east of River Bend. Also at that time, a temporary Army Camp was located there to protect the railroad workers from Indian attacks, and on July 31, 1870, a more permanent military post was located at nearby Cedar Point. New businesses sprang up, most were saloons. In its boom-town days River Bend was said to have had from eleven to twenty saloons, with the railroad crews adding to the already rowdy customer base. Soon most of "old" River Bend moved to the "new" River Bend location, including the post office which operated there until 1942. During the 1870s and 1880s, River Bend was one of the major shipping points for cattle in eastern Colorado.

In 2014, all that remains is the River Bend Cemetery, which sits on a hill overlooking I-70 and the site of River Bend. It is on private property north of the interstate. Legend has it that the River Bend Cemetery was originally established to bury the unfortunate revelers who were shot in gun fights in the various saloons. In addition to the fifty-two marked graves of old time River Bend residents, there are between six and thirteen unmarked graves. These are probably the oldest graves whose markers did not last, or perhaps some were never marked at all because the victims were unknown.

A few of the graves, and the lone tree at River Bend Cemetery

*One of the very old, unmarked graves at River
Bend Cemetery*

Alfred Jessup was a stockman and in partnership in the cattle business with Finis P. Ernest, a well known cattleman in the area, and future son-in-law of cattle baron John Hittson. Jessup had chosen to seek his fortune in the west rather than join his father's firm of Jessup and Moore, paper manufacturers, in Philadelphia. In 1873, young Jessup headed west, he explored California then settled, for a time, on a ranch in New Mexico. Finally he came to Colorado and set himself up with a few head of cattle on a ranch near Deer Trail. One account said that Jessup was a good citizen and generally well liked among cowboys and fellow stockmen, despite his tendency to drink on occasion.

The trouble between the two parties involved in the shoot-out, seemed to have began at the railway station. Oscar Davis, station agent for the Kansas Pacific Railroad, had a quarrel with a young employee and began beating him. Jessup interfered to protect the workman, and an argument ensued between Davis and Jessup. Witnesses said that this discussion went on for quite some time. No one knows for sure who the challenger was, but the two men soon moved out onto a field a few yards from the depot and took positions about one hundred and fifty feet apart. Witnesses also stated that it appeared both parties had been drinking.

No seconds were chosen, as in some duels, but apparently the two had set up some rules and conducted the affair in a somewhat orderly manner. Davis had a Winchester repeating rifle, and Jessup a Colt's Navy Revolver. Each man was to fire three shots. The words, "Are you ready?" repeated by both men was the signal to fire.

Jessup seemed to become nervous at the last moment, and he fired three shots very rapidly without hitting Davis. Davis, who was said to be a crack shot, also missed with his first shot, but he then aimed deliberately, and as his rifle cracked the second time, Jessup threw up his arms, staggered, dropped his pistol, and fell dead. The shot had passed through his heart, killing him instantly.

Several people who had witnessed the act and heard the shots rushed to the scene. Davis coolly helped them to pick up the body of Jessup and carry it back to the station. He refused to give any details about the quarrel that led up to this fight and said only that Jessup was the challenger and was at fault.

A telegram was sent to Jessup's father in Philadelphia. Jessup's body was placed on a train and taken to an undertaker in Denver to await his father's instructions. Jessup's friends said that his father, at this time, was planning a trip west to see his son.

During the confusion following the shooting, Davis slipped out of the crowd, mounted his horse, and disappeared. Although a reward was offered for his capture, Davis was never apprehended. An article in the Denver Tribune in 1878 reported that a man who came to Denver from Deadwood, Dakota Territory, brought news that "Davis, the man that shot Jessup at Deer Trail a couple of years ago, was recently hanged in the Black Hills for horse stealing."

Resources: Colorado Banner, Boulder, July 6, 1876; Colorado Weekly Chieftan, Pueblo, June 15, 1876, Denver Tribune, Oct. 18, 1878; "My River Bend", Irma Kjosness

JUSTICE BY JUDGE LYNCH

What the Law Wouldn't Do . . .

A law was passed in Colorado in 1866 making the hanging of horse thieves illegal. Actually it was not legal before 1866, but was common practice, and continued so for many years. Even though it was illegal, it was more or less condoned in the lawless west during that era. On the sparsely settled prairie, a man's life, as well as his livelihood, may depend on his horse. The theft of horses as well as cattle was a big problem to early settlers. In 1868, the Rocky Mountain News said, "Nothing is so calculated to discourage stock raising as the knowledge that it will be stolen."

Likewise, lynchings were not condemned by the press, nor were they big news. One hanging received only one sentence in the Rocky Mountain News in 1868, "Two deserters, named Charles Watson and Frank Hudson, stole four horses, were followed by the settlers a hundred miles, caught, confessed, and hanged."

At that time, most such thieves were never caught, and those that were spent short stents in jail and then came back to steal again. Hanging served as much more of a deterrent. It not only insured that the dead horse thief would steal no more, it usually made all the other crooks and robbers in the vicinity depart for a less violent neighborhood in which to obtain their livestock.

Although many hangings took place in eastern Colorado, hangings were not commonplace and were usually reserved for the worst kind of criminals. That's where 'Judge Lynch' came in. Making sure that the victim of a hanging deserved what he got, it was said that Judge Lynch had found them guilty. Most every frontier town had some type of vigilance committee. In most cases, some form of kangaroo court would be held, or other means used to get the accused to confess. Criminals had a great fear of Judge Lynch. A report from Sheridan, Kansas said, "A large coil of rope arrived at the depot today marked 'Vigilance Committee,' and immediately there was a stampede of loafers getting out of town."

A hanging took place near Franktown, Colorado in 1870. A twenty-four hour trial was conducted by vigilantes which resulted in confessions from Tom Madison, Frank Cleveland, and Jack Mason that they had stolen forty to sixty horses. Also, charges of cattle theft were brought against them, and they were taken into custody by the local authorities. As the men were being escorted to jail, the sheriff rode alongside a wagon containing the three prisoners and two deputies. A mob of more than twenty-five men surrounded them, threw the sheriff and his men to the ground, and rode off with the prisoners. The sheriff went on to Franktown assuming that the prisoners had just been rescued by their friends. The next morning, when the sheriff set out to recapture them, about fifty yards from where they had been taken, the three men were found hanging from one tree.

Sheriff Alex Barron of Elbert County was similarly unsuccessful in his attempt to prevent a lynching. Fifty masked men overpowered him and took Tip Marion, his brother Joshua, Dick Thompson, and Jerry Wilson from jail to a grove near Middle Kiowa (later became Kiowa) and hanged them in August 1874. Sheriff Barron had arrested the men in possession of stolen horses and mules near Running Creek and Gomer's Mill. Gomer's Mill was located about three miles south of Elbert, Colorado, near County Road 82. After a trial that lasted three days and nights, they were being held at Middle Kiowa jail to appear at the next term of District Court, when they were seized.

The pine tree from which the four men were hanged was located on a hill southeast of Kiowa. It is still known as hangman's point to the old timers in the area. Another version of the story says there was a young boy, age fourteen or sixteen, with the gang of thieves when they were caught. The vigilantes allowed the boy to go say good-by to his horse, and as they hoped, he jumped on his horse and was allowed to escape. They hoped that the scare would make him choose a more legal life style.

In a few cases, murder was as much of a hanging offense as horse theft. During construction of the Kansas Pacific Railroad in 1870, Judge Lynch visited Kit Carson. Milton Straight, a railroad man working on the new water tank, killed Dan O'Connell, a citizen who had come to the tank for water. Straight was arrested and jailed in a makeshift jail in the new town. A mob of about seventy-five men took the jail by storm and hung Straight from the nearby railroad bridge.

In April 1888, five miles north of Burlington, two young surveyors, J. B. McConell and John C. Morrison, were looking up locations on government land. They unknowingly crossed the property of Frederick Baker. Baker rode up to them and ordered them to halt, before they could do so, Baker pulled out a shotgun and shot them both at close range. Baker was taken into custody and put under guard to prevent citizens taking the law into their own hands. How the prisoner was kidnapped is not known, but Baker was taken to Cheyenne Wells and hung from the coal chute near the depot.

"Indian Charley," a half Mexican half Apache, in a drunken fit, stabbed and killed Z. Mills at River Bend on New Year's Eve, 1874. He was arrested and taken to jail in Franktown to await a trial. The jail there was just a small building. The sheriff felt the prisoner was secure there and left him in irons, locked in, and unguarded for the night. When Charley's food was taken in the next morning, the lock had been broken and Charley was gone. He either escaped or was taken away. A search was made and the prisoner was found hanging from a pine tree a short distance east of Franktown.

A horrible murder took place in Fort Collins in April, 1888. J. H. Howe came home intoxicated and found his wife packing to leave him. He went into a rage and stabbed her with a knife. He cut her throat and kicked her out the front door. She ran out the gate and half dozen steps down the street and fell dead. Mr. Howe was arrested and taken to jail. As soon as word of this terrible crime spread, a thousand men gathered at the jail and called for swift justice. The sheriff refused to admit anyone, and finally was able to disperse the crowd. That night, three hundred mounted and armed men, some were masked some were not, overpowered the jail guards, battered down the jail door and obtained the prisoner. Howe was hanged from a derrick which stood near the new courthouse.

Resources: Rocky Mountain News - Dec. 2, 1870, Dec. 4, 1870, Jan. 1, 1874, Jan. 6, 1874, Aug. 27, 1874; "The Hinterland"; Colorado Transcript - Dec. 7, 1870; Colorado Springs Gazette - Aug. 29, 1874; Colorado Daily Chieftain - Aug. 29, 1874; Silver Cliff Rustler -, Apr. 19, 1888; Fort Collins Currier -, Apr. 19, 1888; Castle Rock Journal -, Apr. 11, 1888, "The First Five Years of the Railroad Era in Colorado", by E.O. Davis

JULESBURG CONFRONTATION

The Legend of Jack Slade

Joseph A. Slade, better known as "Jack Slade" was considered an outlaw by some and a hero by others, but he killed many men, some accounts say thirteen, some say twenty-six. He was born in Missouri about 1830. His father died when Jack was four, and some say that caused his unruly behavior starting at a young age. Jack killed his first man at the age of thirteen by hitting him over the head with a rock. It's unclear exactly what led up to the attack, but witnesses said Jack was provoked.

Slade's next killings probably took place while serving in the Army during the Mexican-American War. When the war was over in 1848, he got a job as a teamster with the Central Overland Freight Company. Now Jack's killings consisted of the many Indians and horse thieves who attacked his caravans. This made him a hero with the freight company due to the money and lives he saved by warding off these attacks. He was soon promoted up through management positions until he became division superintendent over the five hundred mile route from Julesburg, Colorado to southwestern Wyoming. This was the Overland route's section most plagued by Indians and outlaws.

Slade's hero façade was somewhat tarnished by his all too frequent bouts with liquor. During these episodes he would sometimes become violent and mean. On a few occasions he would use whatever means necessary to goad men into drawing against him, most of those who did, ended up dead.

In 1857, trouble broke out around Julesburg in the form of frequent robberies. The freight company was missing horses, supplies, and cargo. Overland's stages were being robbed just when they carried money or wealthy passengers. The company suspected an inside job. Jack Slade was asked to go to Julesburg and take over the position of stationmaster.

The man Slade was to replace as stationmaster in Julesburg was Jules Beni, a Frenchman, who the town was named after. Mr. Beni also operated a saloon and ran the town and everyone in it as if he owned them. This earned him a long list of enemies. This list soon included Jack Slade, whose first complaint against Beni was that Jack's drivers were continually getting drunk and in trouble in Jules' establishment and unable to perform their duties. Jack also became convinced that Beni was behind the outbreak of robberies.

Jules had a grudge against Jack for taking his job. When he heard that Slade was suspicious of him in the robberies, Beni knew Slade would come looking for him and he got ready for Slade. When Slade came to Beni's saloon, Jules was waiting behind the door with a shotgun. His first shotgun blast came at close range, through the closed door, hitting Slade. Before Slade fell, Beni had reloaded both barrels and shot him a second time. This time Jack hit the ground, but Beni was still not satisfied, he reloaded and shot him again with both barrels. Then Beni yelled, "Bury him." Thinking Slade was dead, Beni was shocked when Slade lifted his head slightly and told Beni not to worry about his buryn' because he would live long enough to use Beni's ear for a watch guard someday.

Jules Beni's biggest shock came when the citizens of "his" town, after witnessing the incident, became a lynch mob. They grabbed Jules and took him to the nearest tree. The mob didn't have a proper hangman's noose, just a rope, so rather than snapping Beni's neck and killing him instantly, as in a proper hanging, it merely began choking him to death. When Beni had turned blue and was on his last breath, Alexander Benham, superintendent of Holliday Stage Line, arrived by stagecoach and ordered the men to release him. As Jules lay on the ground gasping for breath, the Overland company Superintendent ordered him to leave the Julesburg area and never return. Of course, Jules readily agreed and immediately rode out of town.

Jack Slade was taken to the local doctor, who removed a few of the dozens of buck-shot that riddled his body. The doctor didn't do more because he didn't hold much hope that Slade would survive. When Slade was still alive the next morning, the doctor decided there may be a slight chance for him, but he needed to get to a hospital. The nearest hospital was in Omaha, so Slade endured a most uncomfortable long ride by train. His condition was so bad that he was eventually sent on to St. Louis where he spent a year recuperating in the hospital there.

As soon as Jack was released to return to work, he returned to Julesburg. Beni had never left the area, despite his promise, and the company felt he was still robbing them. There are many versions of exactly how the final confrontation between the two men took place. One story says that after Slade shot Beni and only injured him, he let Beni live long enough to dictate his will, then shot him dead. The fact that is certain is that Jack Slade killed Jules Beni that day. Jack turned himself in to the Military authorities at Fort Laramie, that being the nearest law at that time. Because of what Jack had suffered and because of Beni's criminal reputation, and all accounts saying that it was self defense, Jack would never face any charges for the killing.

Another fact that is pretty widely agreed upon is that Jack cut off both Beni's ears. He carried them in his pocket for a long time and showed them off on occasion, he possibly even used one for a watch guard.

45

Slade's drunken episodes and questionable killing sprees seemed to escalate after that. The Overland Company finally transferred him to a stage station forty miles northwest of Fort Collins. Slade named it Virginia Dale, after his dear wife, who ran the station with him. However his drinking problem didn't improve, even with his wife's influence. It had become such a problem that the Overland Company fired him in 1862.

Jack went to Virginia City, Montana, and started his own freight business, which was short lived due to his usual violent behavior. The first thing he did when he got to town was take a load of lumber from the local mill, even after being told by the owner that he did not extend credit, and would not make an exception for Slade. When Slade was drinking, which was often, he would ride into all the saloons in town and shoot out lamps and anything breakable and just generally push his weight around. In 1864, on one of his drunken rampages, in Virginia City, Montana, a local vigilante group lynched Jack Slade on the gate post of a corral.

Resources: Outlaw Tales of Colorado by Jan Murphy; Estes Park Trail - Sept. 1, 1922; Fort Collins Standard - Apr. 29, 1874; Carbondale Chronicle - Feb. 12, 1900; Denver Post – Sept. 17, 1899, Jan. 11, 1911; Rocky Mountain News – Sept. 19, 1892.

ROUND-UP COOK KILLED AT DEER TRAIL

Reckless and Impetuous

A disagreement that started in the Hays and Watkins' Saloon in Deer Trail on April 23, 1878, resulted in the death of Fritz Kiger, a well known round-up cook. He had cooked for W. H. H. Cramner and other prominent ranchers in the area. Kiger was described as naturally reckless and impetuous, and when aroused by drink, noisy and quarrelsome.

"Fritz the cook," as he was known, and several other men, including Wright Dunham, had been playing cards and drinking freely in the saloon all evening. Wright Dunham was originally from Canada. He was a well known stockman in Colorado and had lived in the Deer Trail area for several years, since it had become the cattle shipping point in Colorado.

A dispute arose between Fritz and Dunham over some point in the game. A bit of a shouting and shoving match took place which resulted in Fritz being put out of the saloon by the bar-keeper. Fritz and Dunham had clashed on a few previous occasions.

As Fritz left the saloon, he called out to Dunham that he'd better get his rifle because he was not afraid of him. Fritz then ran to where he lived and soon returned with a knife in his hand, which he banished around and made violent remarks aimed at Dunham.

Dunham then went and got his rifle and followed Kiger out into the street. When Kiger came at him banishing the knife, Dunham hit him over the head with his rifle. Fritz staggered backwards then stooped over like a person about to pick something up. At this, Dunham struck Fritz a second time on the back of the head. Fritz fell to the ground unconscious.

Dunham stood and looked at his victim for a moment, and when he didn't move, Dunham panicked and ran to his hotel. In his room, he grabbed a few things and headed for the stables. The stable door was locked, so he broke the lock and went in and rapidly saddled his horse. He was about to mount and ride away when he just stopped, left his horse standing in the barn, and walked to the Deer Trail House and delivered himself to Justice C. E. Porter, confessing what he had done.

Fritz Kiger died the next morning, after never regaining consciousness. Fritz was forty-three years old.

A dispatch was sent notifying the Sheriff's office about the affair. Coroner McHatten was notified, and along with Deputy Sheriff Arnold, took the Kansas Pacific train to Deer Trail. Upon arrival, McHatten summoned a jury composed of six local men; Lee Gould, Ewell Brown, Abram Brown, Henry Gould, W. J. Lampen, and G. A. Williams. The body was viewed, witnesses examined, and a verdict was returned that the deceased came to his death from wounds received at the hands of Wright Dunham. Sheriff Arnold took Dunham to jail in Denver, where he was held without bail, to await trial on the charge of first degree murder.

Wright Dunham was tried in the Arapahoe County District Court in October, 1878. He was found guilty of murder and sentenced to life in the Colorado State Penitentiary at Canon City. His appeal to the Colorado Supreme Court in 1881 was denied. Dunham was pardoned by executive order of Governor

Job A. Cooper on December 24, 1889, after serving eleven years.

Dunham, who was forty-nine when he committed the crime, had just lost his wife the previous year. He was sixty years old when released from prison. He had two daughters in Missouri, and two sons at Deer Trail.

Resources: Colorado Weekly Chieftain - May 2, 1878, October 24, 1878; Rocky Mountain News – Jan. 28, 1879; Colorado State Penitentiary.

ELBERT COUNTY GANG OF DESPERADOES

Wilder and Hall . . . . . the Leaders

In the spring of 1875, the citizens of Elbert County were demanding that the authorities take action to clean up the gang of desperadoes who had been stealing, bullying, and generally running rough shod over the area for several months.

The leaders of the gang were Evan E. Hall and William H. Wilder who had come to the area to work at Gomer's sawmill, located south of Elbert, six miles from Bijou Basin and fifteen miles from Kiowa, on the edge of the Black Forest.

Hall soon entered into a more lucrative business, that of whiskey selling and gambling. He enticed the mill hands and wood choppers to his place and many experienced heavy gambling losses. Hall then forced them to sign papers drawing on their employer P. P. Gomer for their debts. Finally, he confronted Gomer with the papers saying Gomer owed him $3,000. Gomer refused to pay and was threatened by Hall. Gomer, who lived in Denver, didn't return to his mill for seven months out of fear.

The gang had people so intimidated that gang members felt themselves above the law. Hall once stopped at the Twelve Mile House to have a drink. A local rancher came in to ask for his mail. For no reason, Hall pulled his gun on the man and said, "No you don't need your mail." Fortunately, a bystander knocked the gun out of Hall's hand, and when further threatened and alone, Hall departed. Wilder once held a gun on a young man and disarmed him while Hall cracked his head open with his pistol handle. The boy did survive the nearly fatal wound. Hall killed a man named Peterson, who supposedly was Hall's partner in the ranching business, in one of his bullying episodes. Due to threats against witnesses and the general fear with which he was regarded, Hall was not prosecuted for this crime.

As most of the gang members were wanted on various charges in various locations, Elbert County issued warrants for about a dozen men. Hall and Wilder were also wanted on warrants in Arapahoe County. A reward of $300, by Elbert County and $400 by P. P. Gomer was offered for the arrest of Hall and Wilder. On March 26, Deputy Sheriff Hooker from Kiowa and a posse of fifteen men proceeded to the sawmill and arrested eight members of the gang. Unfortunately, Hall and Wilder weren't among them. Earlier that day, Hall and Wilder had set out for Denver, where they planned to confront Gomer and collect their $3,000 from him. The eight prisoners were taken back to Kiowa and housed in a store, guarded by citizens armed with rifles and shot-guns.

When Hall and Wilder reached Twelve Mile House, they learned that Gomer had passed through there the previous day heading for Kiowa. Figuring that he may be headed to the mill, Hall and Wilder turned and headed back. When they reached the mill, they discovered eight of their men had been captured. They sent messages to Gomer in Kiowa, saying that unless the men were freed and the money paid to them, they would kill him. They also threatened to kill fifty of the best men in the county if their men were not released.

The next day, Deputy Hooker and posse went back to the mill to arrest Hall and Wilder. They reached the mill just at twilight. J. H. Hooker, father of the deputy sheriff, an old and much respected citizen, accompanied by another man, circled around within a few feet of the concealed Hall and Wilder. Hooker called to them to surrender and throw down their weapons. Hall drew his gun, but Hooker leveled his shotgun and fired first. He was wheeling to retreat, when a shot from Hall's revolver struck him in the back. Hooker ran ten steps and turned and fired again. Hall dropped to his knees and fired two shots, both hitting Hooker in the chest. Hooker died twenty minutes later.

Hall and Wilder mounted and rode rapidly away into the pines. They were pursued by the posse, but they easily escaped in the darkness. They stayed in the timber as they headed in the direction of Colorado Springs. Hall had been hit by both of Hooker's bullets and was in pain and becoming weak from loss of blood. When they reached Colorado Springs on April 2, Hall turned himself in to the sheriff. Hall knew he needed medical attention, and figured he'd be safe from his pursuers while he recuperated. He also thought that El Paso County couldn't hold him for long as they had no charges against him. Wilder chose not to surrender and moved on, but was captured a few days later behind Pikes Peak, and joined Hall in the El Paso County jail.

They were held there until the grand jury met on April 21. Both Elbert and Arapahoe County had warrants for the prisoners. Hall and Wilder had convinced the jury that their lives would be in danger if returned to Elbert County. So the grand jury turned them over to Arapahoe County and they were sent to jail in Denver.

On July 26, 1875, seven of the most desperate prisoners escaped from the Denver jail by filing through the bars and overpowering two guards. Among the seven were Hall and Wilder, and a friend named Leighton, who was the instigator of the jail break. Governor Routt put up an additional reward of $200 each for the escaped prisoners.

The three men headed back into the familiar pines country where they were more easily hidden. They moved around, staying in different locations each night. One day they came to the house of Sam Dyer, who, either out of complacency, or fear of these men, gave them food and let them stay in an old cabin on his place. They would hunt in the woods in the daytime and return there at night.

The officers and posse who were looking for Hall and Wilder made it a habit to watch the few homesteads in the area, knowing that Hall and Wilder might eventually approach one and ask for provisions. They noticed some activity at Sam Dyer's place. They approached Dyer in the daytime when the escapees were not around and questioned him. Dyer said the fugitives wanted him to help find them horses, but so far he had refused. Dyer then agreed to help set a trap by telling the men that he would get them horses and they could go to some corrals near an unoccupied home a few miles away to get them the next day.

When the three outlaws arrived at the corrals, the posse opened fire. All three men were hit. Hall and Leighton dropped. Leighton never moved again, but Hall got back up and was running beside Wilder before he realized it. However, after a few hundred yards, Hall stopped and told Wilder he was shot full of holes and couldn't go on. Hall asked Wilder to get some opium out of his pants pocket and give it to him for the pain. Then he insisted Wilder leave him and make his escape, which Wilder did. Hall was found and taken prisoner by the posse, he was made comfortable and died in a few hours.

Wilder, who had been hit in the arm and was also in some pain by this time, was becoming weak from loss of blood. At daylight Wilder came to a ranch near Monument Station owned by a man named Bob Watson. Wilder told the man that he had escaped from jail and that there was a reward for him. He said if Watson would give him a meal and take him to Denver he could collect the reward. The ranchman gave him a good meal but declared that he could not spare the time to take him to Denver and was not in the man catching business. Watson let him spend the night in his granary, gave him food the next morning and told him to go camp out down by Monument creek until his wound healed and then he could get out of the country.

Wilder had just settled in by the creek and was enjoying bathing his wound with the cool water, when he was spotted by two men. Wilder didn't have time or the strength to put up a resistance and was taken into custody by the posse. He was taken to Denver to jail.

Leighton's real name was Jerome Berry. He told Wilder that he had killed his wife in Mississippi many years ago, and been on the run every since. He had killed five men in various states. He claimed all had been in self defense. He had gone to the penitentiary for one murder, but had broken out. He, in fact, had broken out of many jails, and once escaped from a wagon which was hauling him to jail.

William H. Wilder was charged with accessory to the murder of Joshua Hooker at Gomer's Mill, south of Elbert, Colorado. He was tried in Elbert County on December 9, 1875. The jury turned in a verdict of not guilty. Everyone involved seemed satisfied with the verdict. The guilty man had already received his punishment.

Resources: Colorado Daily Chieftain, Dec 11, 1875, Mar. 27, 1875; Rocky Mountain News, Aug. 10, 1875, Aug. 8, 1875, Apr. 16, 1875, May 26, 1875; Las Animas Leader, Apr. 2, 1875; Denver Daily Times, Aug. 9, 1875; Colorado Transcript, Aug. 4, 1875.

TREASURE AT CLIFFORD, COLORADO

Fact or Legend ?

Clifford School House, 2010, one-quarter mile off Highway 287. About all that's left in the ghost town of Clifford, Colorado.

An interesting story of buried treasure is told about Clifford, Colorado. A gang of bandits who stole about one hundred thousand dollars in an army payroll robbery in 1862 are supposed to have buried the loot in the area east of Clifford.

Clifford, Colorado, is now a ghost town located between Hugo and Boyero on the eastern plains of Colorado. It was once a stage station on the Smokey Hill Trail.

There was a gang of eight outlaws who had "retired" on the plains of Colorado after committing numerous robberies in California in 1847. They had been living quiet lives as farmers and cattle ranchers in the Hugo/Clifford area. Evidently by 1862 their funds were running low and one of them got a tip about a poorly guarded U. S. Army payroll headed for Denver by stagecoach. They decided to pull one final robbery and then move on east to Chicago.

The robbery went bad when they discovered that the stagecoach was not poorly guarded at all, but accompanied by four armed guards. They got the payroll but only two of the gang survived the chase and shoot-out that followed. A posse was quickly formed and went out after the remaining two.

In order to make better time and not get caught with the money, the two bandits stopped and buried it east of Clifford. They dug three shallow trenches and packed the dirt on top to look like graves. A rock resembling a tombstone was placed on each mound. On two of the stones they carved their names and the year 1847. On the third stone they carved "unknown." Perhaps they wanted people to think some unknown person had gunned them down and got killed doing it. In the center of the graves, they dug a large hole and buried the money in three Dutch Ovens. Then the two outlaws disappeared and were never caught.

In about 1884, twenty-two years after the robbery, long after the hunt for the robbers had been abandoned, a stranger from Chicago stopped at James Will's sheep ranch, near Clifford. He stayed several days and mostly just walked around on the prairie east of town. He then seemed to give up finding whatever he was looking for. He never told James Will who he was but he told him the story of the robbery and the two surviving bandits and the graves.

The wild tale was told around for years but neither James Will nor most of Clifford's residents put much stock in the tale until

May 1931, when George Elkins found a stone inscribed "1847." There were also words carved on the stone, but time had made them impossible to read. This brought new life to the story. People searched and dug all over the area where the stone was found, but found nothing.

In 1934, another stone was found by Tom Hatton. This stone read, "D. Grover and Joseph Fox-Lawe – Aug. 8, 1847." Another rash of searching and digging took place with no result.

Most people believe that the stranger who visited James Will in 1884 was one of the robbers and actually found the money and took it with him when he left. He then scattered the stones around to keep people guessing and digging for years. That is why, before he left, he felt safe telling Mr. Will the whole story of how and where the treasure had been buried. There are, of course, others who think it is still out there somewhere. They think that the 1884 visitor probably was one of the bandits, but that he gave up and left without the treasure.

There are many buried treasure stories and most should be taken with a grain of salt, especially after one hundred and fifty years. Another mysterious cache of gold was found in the nearby town of Wild Horse. Wild Horse burned to the ground in 1917. A charred keg containing gold coins was found in or close to the burned ruins of the old Albany Hotel. Nothing is known about where the gold came from and how it ended up in Wild Horse.

Resources: The Story Museum of James M. Deem by James Deem; Guide to Treasure in Colorado by H. Glenn Carson

DEN OF THIEVES

Found at Kit Carson

Kit Carson, Colorado was named after the old frontiersman and Army Scout who died at nearby Fort Lyons in 1868. Kit Carson rose from ashes three times, each time changing its location slightly.

The Kansas Pacific Railroad was completed to Kit Carson on March 28, 1870. The town of Kit Carson had been established prior to the arrival of the railroad, and had big plans to become a major hub of commerce. A long article from Kit Carson extolled the advantages it would have over Sheridan, Kansas, the Kansas Pacific Railroad terminus at that time.

This prediction came to pass, at least for a short time. Kit Carson became the new terminus and "end of track" for about four months in 1870. Trains would arrive there from Kansas City and passengers would complete the hundred and fifty mile trip to Denver by stagecoach. Passengers would arrive in Kit Carson by stage from Denver and board the train for Kansas City. Denver reported nine hundred ninety-four passengers arriving by stagecoach from the east in the month of April 1870. With various lag times between connections, plus hoards of railroad workers, business was booming. The maximum population of Kit Carson in 1870 was fifteen hundred, and fifty houses were being built at a time. It was named the seat of Greenwood County.

Of course, with this boom also came the bad element which tended to follow money. Kit Carson became a wild west town in the true sense of the word. A reporter in the Denver Daily Times, undoubtedly being sarcastic, said "The town of Kit Carson holds a stronger inducement for a coffin maker who can turn out work rapidly, than any other city on the plains."

In May 1870, Indian trouble sprang up around Kit Carson. Eleven track graders for the railroad were killed and nineteen injured west of Carson, numerous head of livestock were stolen, and the water tank four miles east of Carson was torn down by Indians. Railroad workers were immediately armed and troops were sent from Fort Lyons, Colorado, and Fort Wallace and Fort Hays in Kansas, to patrol the area. About this same time, railroad construction west out of Kit Carson was resumed.

Shortly after the railroad reached Lake Station, a few miles east of where Limon is now located, on July 10, 1870. Stage service to Kit Carson was discontinued and connections were made at Lake Station. Kit Carson's boom came to an end. The population dwindled down to just a few businessmen and residents. Many houses were moved to West Las Animas. Hopes were kept high by talk of a Kansas Pacific spur line to Las Animas.

The Arkansas Valley Railroad was finally built between Kit Carson and Las Animas in 1873, bringing new life to the town. This, too, was short lived. The spur was shut down in the fall of 1877. A roundhouse was maintained at Kit Carson until 1878. An engine was kept there to help trains up the First View hill. First View is between Cheyenne Wells and Kit Carson and was on a high enough rise that on a clear day it offered the first view of the Rocky Mountains, coming from the east.

In 1876, the Kansas Pacific Railroad had been concerned for some time with the mysterious disappearance of railroad cargo. They had not been able to pinpoint the problem and it was growing gradually worse. In January of 1877, they hired the Rocky Mountain Detective Association, from Denver, to investigate. Detectives narrowed it down to the Kit Carson area and sent an undercover agent there to snoop around.

The investigation soon revealed that because Carson was at the foot of a steep grade, heavy laden box cars were often laid over there. A ring of thieves had been at work helping themselves to cargo off these side-tracked cars. At first it was just food or useful items then gradually expanded to high priced items and finally even to livestock. It became apparent that a railroad watchman named Frank Williamson was in on it or was being paid off.

After putting this all together, the detective decided to take action. He went to the magistrate at Kit Carson, whose name was Pat Shanley, to get warrants for the arrest of several people he suspected. Shanley was also the proprietor of the hotel. Mr. Shanley introduced him to the constable, named Worth Keene, who was also proprietor of the saloon. The men in the saloon began to act strange and some of the men he had warrants for began to disappear. The detective got a strong feeling that he was in danger. When the next train came through for Kansas City, he quietly stepped aboard and was not seen again.

With Shanley and Keene now on the suspect list, a second agent, McLean, was sent. He was actually accepted by the town for a while because he had a lot of money and spent it freely. When word reached the agency that McLean was suspected as an agent, he was telegraphed to return to Denver immediately. He caught the next train. Just prior to leaving, he telegraphed Denver that the watchman, Williamson had left town on the train just ahead of his.

Williamson's train was met in Denver. He was on board with his baggage checked for Montana, and was taken into custody. As soon as McLean was back in Denver, a special train was sent to Kit Carson to make the arrests. Faced with six armed officers, the suspects had little choice but to surrender. A total of eight more men were arrested, including the ring leaders, Shanley and Keene. A hurried search was made of the vicinity, and a large quantity of stolen goods were found hidden, mostly buried, for four miles down the railroad as well as two miles east and north along the creeks.

Because the population of Kit Carson had decreased so much when the railroad moved on, there were only about twenty-five permanent residents at this time. When the nine men were taken to jail, it left Kit Carson almost a ghost town, consisting mostly of women and children.

The prisoners were taken to jail in West Las Animas and bail set. Three of the men were sent to the penitentiary for long terms, and four escaped on technicalities. Shanley, Keene, and one other forfeited their bonds and disappeared from the state and were never apprehended. What happened to their families left in Kit Carson is unknown. It is known that Kit Carson did not die but rose from the ashes once again.

Resources: Colorado Weekly Chieftan, May 19. 1870, Feb. 8,1877, Mar. 29, 1877; Denver Daily Tribune, Feb. 2, 1877; Denver Daily Times, June 19, 1873; "Hands Up", by David J. Cook; "The First Five Years of The Railroad Era in Colorado", E.O. Davis.

MURDERER ARRESTED
IN DEER TRAIL

A Very Dangerous Killer

On the twenty-second of April 1877, a man named George Wilson went into a saloon in Deer Trail, and apparently having been drinking there or in other saloons most all day, began shooting out the lights and breaking up everything in the place. When the bar keeper could not control him or quiet him down, he sent for the law.

Wilson was taken into custody, fortunately without gunplay. He was taken to Denver and turned over to Sheriff Cook, who recognized him as the man who was wanted for killing Sheriff Tafoya of Trinidad, Colorado, five years previously. It was discovered that he was also wanted for killing a deputy sheriff in Texas over a year past.

Sheriff Cook took him down to Trinidad, where he was positively identified as the man wanted there. Since it was determined that the Trinidad jail may not have been sufficient to hold such a known desperate criminal, he was taken to Pueblo for safe keeping until his trial. In June, George Wilson was among several prisoners who over powered a guard and made their escape from the Pueblo jail. Texas authorities offered a reward of $750, and Las Animas County a reward of $300 for his re-capture, to no avail.

The events that led up to the killing of Sheriff Tafoya in February of 1872, were similar to his behavior in Deer Trail. Wilson and a party of Texas herders were in Trinidad. Wilson was in a saloon drinking and gambling when he declared that he had been robbed of six or seven dollars. He became rowdy, and the bartender even offered to make up the money he'd supposedly lost. Wilson would not be placated. He left and soon returned with his brother, Fayette Wilson and three others.

After it had escalated to this point, Sheriff Tafoya stepped up to Wilson and uttered some warning words. In an instant, Wilson pulled his gun and shot Tafoya in the head at close range, and killed him instantly. The place erupted in gunfire and wild confusion took hold. Everyone in the saloon ran out into the street. The Texas men went to the stable to saddle their horses and make their escape. In the meantime an enraged crowd was gathering. The Texans were heavily armed and able to keep the mob at a safe distance.

As soon as their horses were saddled, they rode out of town, followed by the angry crowd. Constable Young and several other local pursuers were shot while trying to stop the band of Texas cowboys from escaping. Apparently, none fatally, as later reports stated that Tafoya was the only one killed in the melee. Coroner Witt of Las Animas County, telegraphed to Fort Union, New Mexico, for assistance. It was dispatched.

Wilson and his small band must have rode swiftly back to Texas and probably disbanded, because they were never seen nor captured. Wilson, however, was up to his old tricks in 1876 in Montague County Texas. Deputy Sheriff William Broadus arrested Wilson on charges of being connected with some shooting affair in that county and took him to jail in Montague. On arrival there, Wilson requested his handcuffs be removed so that he could wash his hands. Foolishly, Broadus did so. Immediately, Wilson grabbed a pistol that happened to be within reach, shot the deputy dead, and made his escape. He then remained at large until the Deer Trail episode, which he also escaped from in June of 1877.

The next sighting of Wilson was on October 15, 1877 in Prescott, Arizona. Wilson and a companion named Reb Fellos, also a wanted thief and murder from Texas, attempted to shoot up and take over the town of Prescott. The sheriff was called upon to arrest the two men. Wilson, of course, refused to give up peaceably and got into a gun fight with the sheriff. The sheriff, in the performance of his duty, was obliged to shoot both men, killing Fellos and mortally wounding Wilson, who died a short time later.

Resources: Colorado Weekly Chieftain, May 10, 1877, May 17, 1877, Nov. 1, 1877; Daily Register Call, Feb. 17, 1872; Rocky Mountain News, Feb. 3, 1982; Denver Daily Times, June 7, 1877.

PERSISTENCE OF A LAWMAN

Ruled – Self Defence

J. W. Barron, while working for the Rocky Mountain Detective Association, hunted, trailed, and finally brought in a wanted murderer, who had been eluding him for four years. Frank Porter was arrested by Barron in Washington Territory and brought back to Denver in March of 1882 for the murder of George Short, which took place near Hugo, Colorado, in 1878.

Barron had been sheriff of Hugo at the time of the murder and investigated the case. Shortly after that he was elected Sheriff of Elbert County, and since the crime took place in Elbert County, again worked on finding the killer, but with no luck. Barron later joined the Rocky Mountain Detective Association. Headquartered in Denver, the Rocky Mountain Detective Association was well known, during this era, for capturing many criminals that other understaffed law enforcement agencies of the time could not.

When Barron and his prisoner got off the train in Denver, Porter was secured by a strange set of chains. Laboring under the impression that since the prisoner was a desperate murderer, and had been eluding the law for four years, Barron assumed that he would likely take any possible chance to escape. Therefore, before departing Washington, Barron had a blacksmith make a pair of crude hand cuffs, which were securely riveted onto the prisoner. He also had an iron band riveted around Porter's waist, to which was attached a heavy log chain, which in turn was connected to the log chain between the hand cuffs.

The following morning Barron took his prisoner on to Kiowa where he was placed in the Elbert County jail. At that time, a blacksmith was called to remove the chains from Frank Porter.

Frank Porter had been employed as a cowboy on the Fine P. Ernest ranch near Hugo in 1878 when the killing occurred. George Short did the same work for R. G. Webster. They met up when the two crews got together on a round-up. The two had known each other previously because they came from the same area in Missouri. There may have been ill feelings between them from the past. Frank was nineteen years old at the time, and George was many years older. It seemed that George was always teasing and needling Frank about something, often turning into harsh words between them.

The day of the killing, George was mocking Frank in front of the men. Frank answered him back in the same mocking way, which made the men laugh. George got angry and told Frank he would kick him clear across the country. He pulled off his jacket and started toward Frank. Because he was much older and bigger than Frank, Frank knew George could whip him, and as angry as he was, he'd probably whip him good. So Frank grabbed a stick of fire wood from the nearby wood pile. As George came toward him, Frank raised the stick as a threat. Instead of stopping, George went to the wood pile to get himself a stick. Frank knew he was really in for a beating if George got after him with a stick. When George reached for the stick, Frank hit him over the head. George fell unconscious, and died a short time later.

Frank was as shocked as everyone else that the blow had killed George, as he had not intended to do anything but defend himself. But he decided he had better leave the country just in case. Frank took Fine Ernest's horse back and turned him out, and took off on foot. He knew he would likely get in more trouble for stealing a horse than for killing somebody. No one seemed to blame Frank for what happened and no one tried to stop him.

When Frank got to Deer Trail, apparently a friend of his, who worked for John Hittson, lent him an old sorrel horse. After working for awhile in Cheyenne, Wyoming, Frank had enough money to make it to Washington Territory where his parents lived. That is where he remained for the rest of the four years until apprehended by Barron.

During Barron's investigation as Elbert County Sheriff, he had discovered this fact about Hittson's sorrel horse disappearing about the same time as Porter and always thought it might be a lead. Then over a year later, while on the trail of another criminal, Barron stayed one night at a cow camp. There were known friends of Porters among the cowboys there. After they thought Barron was asleep, he heard one of the cowboys remark, "that old sorrel horse has finally returned from the Pacific Northwest." This was Barron's first clue to the whereabouts of Porter. He spent another three years following up on that clue, with hundreds of letters and telegrams, until he finally made the three thousand mile trip and got his man.

Frank Porter's father had hired a Denver attorney to represent his son. He accompanied Frank to Kiowa. At his preliminary hearing, after the facts of the case were presented, bail of $3,000 was set and the case was continued for a year. Frank returned home to Washington. When he came back for the scheduled trial a year later it was again continued for another year. Frank's bail was reduced to $1,500, and he again returned to Washington.

Finally, on his third trip to Elbert County court, Frank's trial took place before a jury of his peers. After Frank told his story to the jury, and it was corroborated by other witnesses, the jury returned a verdict of not guilty by reason of self defense. After a brief stay with friends at Deer Trail, Frank Porter returned to Washington a free man.

Instead of being a hero for all his hard work and persistence, J. W. Barron was criticized for wasting time and money in pursuing what turned out to be such a petty criminal for such a long time.

Resources: Rocky Mountain News – Mar. 9, 1882, Mar. 12, 1882, Mar. 12, 1884, Mar. 11, 1884, Denver Daily Tribune – June 29, 1878.

DEER TRAIL RANCHER
FOUND FROZEN

Long Trip Home

Ruie Middlemist had been worried sick for nearly a week. Her husband, Alex, had gone to River Bend for a load of grain and should have been back days ago. There were many dangers that he could have encountered in that wild country on that fifty mile round trip. Ranch employees set out on February 18, 1881, in search of their boss, Walter Alexander (Alex) Middlemist. They found him that day, and were faced with a gruesome sight that they likely never forgot.

Somewhere along the twenty-five mile trail between the Middlemist Ranch and River Bend they found Mr. Middlemist's frozen body face down on the ground beside his wagon. He had last been seen leaving River Bend at ten a.m. five days earlier, on the thirteenth, with his four horse team pulling a wagon load of grain. The weather was clear that morning, but extremely cold. There was a light covering of snow on the ground.

From what the searchers found at the scene, they theorized that Alex must have had a heart attack or apoplexy (what we now call a stroke). It is unknown if this was ever confirmed. His body lay just as if he had fallen from the wagon seat. He had an expression of agony on his face. He was probably dead when he hit the ground as there was no sign of any movement. The reins were still in one hand, the other hand was raised as if to protect his face. His hat had come off and laid a few feet away. His faithful half-shepherd half-mastiff dog was laying close by his side as if to keep him warm.

Having a grip on the reins, even in death, must have kept the team from moving from the spot where the tragedy occurred. The two wheel horses stood, looking petrified, they were frozen to death. The two fore horses lay on their sides in the snow barely breathing. There was also a saddle horse tied to the wagon that was in bad shape but still standing. All the flesh was gone from the front legs of the two dead horses. It was surmised that that was probably what kept the poor dog alive while he stayed by his master's side. If it had been wolves or coyotes, they would not have stopped with that small portion of only the dead animals.

Alex Middlemist was a well known and wealthy rancher east of Deer Trail and north of River Bend. He was born in New York in 1842, and came west with three of his brothers, William B., James, and Andrew, first to Kansas and then to Colorado. He died at the age of thirty-nine, leaving a wife, who was pregnant, and two small children. Alex married Zeruia (Ruie) Hager in 1877, and at the time of his death his son Andrew E. was two years old and Allen David was one. Following Alex's untimely death, his wife apparently returned to Missouri where her parents lived, because a third son, Walter Alexander, was born in Missouri in August of 1881.

The devastated search party unhooked the dead horses from the wagon and hitched up others, loaded the body of their boss on top of the grain sacks and took Alex to River Bend. From there, he was taken by train to Deer Trail, where the coroner ruled his death was accidental. His body was later taken on into Denver for burial, accompanied by deputy sheriff, Amos Cantley, of Deer Trail.

Resources: Rocky Mountain News, February 20, 1881; Leadville Daily Herald, Feb. 20, 1881; family history, Kathy Middlemist Currier.

NEWTON VORCE

The Deer Trail Desperado

*Newt Vorce, in back row, in
Denver with a group of Deer Trail
Cowboys, early 1900s.*

Much has been written and published about Newt Vorce. Many newspapers called him the "Deer Trail Terror" or the "Deer Trail Desperado." His obituary called him "one of the more picturesque of the early-day frontiersmen and gun fighters whose exploits helped make history when the west was young." It was also said that he was well liked and not feared by people he worked for, or the folks who knew him that lived around Deer Trail and Byers.

Newton Vorce is believed to have been born in Berkley County, Virginia, around 1840. It seems every record found of him lists a different date and place of birth. It is believed that he may have been orphaned at a young age and did not know his exact date of his birth. The 1850 US Census lists Newton, age 10, with his family in Michigan. His father Wm. and mother Marabee, and nine siblings, ranging from age twenty to age one. The 1860 Census lists Newton Vorce, age 21, living with D. D. and Sarah Wallace in Michigan. It lists his occupation as "stage driver." Vorce does not appear on another Census until 1900 where he is listed as an employee of Mary Collier in Byers, age 61 (*birth year 1839*), and then in 1920, in Weld County, Colorado, age 87, (*birth year 1833*).

Newt enlisted in the army in August of 1865, a few months after the end of the Civil War. That record shows him to be 18 years old (*birth year 1847*). He served in the Second Calvary, K Company. He was four foot nine inches tall, and was a bugler. He was discharged in 1868, at Fort Sanders, Dakota Territory, after completing his three years service.

He came to Colorado shortly after that, and worked on ranches in the Deer Trail and Eastern Colorado area the rest of his life. It is believed that some of the first ranches he worked on were those of John Hittson, W.H.H. Cramner, Fine Ernest, and Charlie Rhodes.

Newt Vorce's life of crime seemed to have begun in the early spring of 1887, when he was arrested for horse stealing and sentenced to the Arapahoe County jail for nine months. Evidently this arrest also included an altercation with a deputy. The first of June he escaped and went back to Deer Trail to visit his girlfriend, Mollie Collier, a grass widow who had lived in Deer Trail for several years.

Six months later, on December 7, Deputy Sheriff Amos Cantley came to Deer Trail with a warrant for Vorce's arrest for horse stealing and breaking jail. There was a story that said the reason Cantley didn't come after Vorce for six months, when everyone knew he had been in Deer Trail all that time, was that Cantley owed Vorce some money and Vorce had been trying to collect.

When Deputy Cantley got to Deer Trail, he was told that Vorce was at the creek cutting wood. Cantley deputized Ned Hanks and they went after Vorce. They saw his wagon heading back to town as they rode out. When they approached and informed Newt they had a warrant for his arrest, Newt got down between the team of horses. Vorce said if they wanted him they'd have to come get him. A shoot out took place. When it was over, both the horses were dead and Sheriff Cantley had been hit in the arm, breaking it at the elbow. Newt ran 200 yards to Mrs. Beatty's house and barricaded himself inside, no one was home. Cantley and Hanks returned to town to take care of Cantley's arm. After sending a telegram to Denver for help, Hanks recruited more men and went back after Vorce. As they were approaching Mrs. Beatty's place, they saw her and her daughter returning in their buggy. Before the posse could get there, Newt came out of the house and cut the harness, stole the buggy horse and made his escape.

On the train that arrived from Denver the next day was a Doctor for Cantley, and Undersheriff Chivington with four other officers, plus guns and ammunition. Cantley was in worse shape than they thought. The Doctor removed several bone chips and set the arm the best he could, then Cantley was taken by train to the hospital in Denver for further care. A year and a half after this incident, Cantley was arrested for cattle stealing.

It is believed that Mollie Collier got Vorce a horse and helped him escape in the night. The posse searched the area all day with no clues. For the three months since his escape, Vorce would spend nights at Mollie's house and then head for the woods early in the morning to hide out. Mollie's daughter, Charity, would take him food. Mollie was later taken to jail for assisting him.

Newt traveled down Muddy Creek and arrived in Corona (approximately twelve miles west of Fort Morgan) at 10 p.m. on December 8. He stayed at Ben Brewer's ranch, five miles from Corona that night. He left the next morning heading for Antelope flats, (about twenty miles south of Corona), with the intention of returning to Brewer's to spend the night. He was armed with a Winchester and two revolvers, and was mounted on a fine gray horse, which was evidence of Vorce's superior judgment in stealing horses.

Undersheriff Frank Hollingsworth arrived at Corona on the 11:55 train. Vorce had been discovered hiding out in a dugout on the L.H.C. ranch, formerly owned by Lyman H. Cole, situated twelve miles south of Corona. There were seven dugouts along a bank; Vorce was in the fourth one from the south with a sheepherder named Billy and three other unknown men. Frank Hollingsworth and a posse, including his brother Gay Hollingsworth, surrounded the dugout. They had the men pinned down in the dugout for hours, Vorce and the others returning fire. When Vorce saw what was happening, he told Billy he'd better throw up his hands and get out before things got bad. Billy went out with hands in the air and yelled "Don't shoot." Gay Hollingsworth, thinking it was Vorce surrendering, headed toward him. Gun fire erupted and Gay was shot and killed. As confusion broke out and concern shifted to taking care of the dead man, Newt and the others escaped.

He was on the loose for a week. People believed he was in New Mexico by this time. On December 17th cowboys who had

74

discovered Vorce hiding in a dugout on the Robinson ranch twelve miles west of Deer Trail, telegraphed Denver. Colonel Chivington and Deputy Lynd arrived at Deer Trail the next day and got a posse together. Two wagon loads of men left Deer Trail and arrived at the dugout at eight o'clock that evening. When they arrived at the Robinson ranch and had the dugout surrounded, a sheepherder named Lathrop, came out to get water wearing Vorce's hat and coat. The officers, thinking it was Vorce, fired and the sheepherder was killed. He laid where he fell for several hours as it was right in the line of fire. Finally 'Scotty' and Robinson, who were known by Vorce and the other men in the dugout, went out and retrieved the body. They were not fired upon.

Colonel Chivington set off dynamite near the dugout and started a fire with brush on the roof of the dugout. This caused smoke to enter the dugout, causing Vorce to surrender.

Vorce was taken to Deer Trail in a wagon. They sent for a special train, and took him back to Denver. Vorce, who had received only a scratch when a bullet grazed his neck, was so peaceful when arrested that he was allowed to make the trip without shackles or hand cuffs. He was kept in the Arapahoe County jail on $1,500 bail, on charges of assault with intent to murder. The killing of Hollingsworth took place in Weld County; Vorce would face charges there for second degree murder.

The coroner's report said that Hollingsworth was killed with two bullets from different caliber guns, and that Vorce probably fired one of them. That was good enough for the jury when he was tried in Greeley, found guilty, and sentenced to 14 years in the State Penitentiary. His prison record of 1888 says he was 47 years old, (*which makes him born in 1841*) in Martinsburg, VA.

Newt, however, served only five years of that sentence. It was the custom of that time, for the governor to grant a full pardon to two prisoners per year, chosen by the warden, for exemplary conduct. On New Year's Day, 1893, Governor Routt pardoned Newton Vorce, and he was released.

A few months later, in April 1893, Vorce shot at, harassed and assaulted a salesman in a Byers saloon for refusing to shake his hand. The bartender and others subdued Vorce long enough to allow the unfortunate fellow to escape.

On July 2, 1893, Vorce was the cook on a horse roundup for the F.F. Carrol outfit. He, and several other cowboys, apparently fell out with the captain of the roundup and headed into Evans, Colorado. They had a few drinks and started shooting out the town lights. Vorce took objection to Marshal Huff trying to call him down. Vorce put his six-shooter to Huff's chest and pulled the trigger. Huff's life was saved by the fact that Vorce had used up all his ammunition on the street lights. A scuffle ensued, blows were exchanged, and it was ended when Vorce struck Huff over the head with his gun, inflicting a serious wound. He and his companions immediately rode out of town, shooting out all the street lights as they went.

As before, Vorce managed to elude the lawmen who were after him for several days. However, on July 6th, he was discovered in a sheepherders shack ten miles north of Hardin, twenty-five miles east of Greeley. Sheriff Arthur and Undersheriff Knowlton rode out there and deputized cowboys, Elmer Shadomy and Bill Cook. They found Vorce sleeping on the floor of the shack. Bill Cook got a loop over one of Vorce's feet and dragged him out of the cabin where he was placed in shackles and taken back to Greeley. Vorce was tried and found guilty on the charge of "assault with intent to murder." He was sentenced to ten years in the State Penitentiary.

Vorce served a little over six years of that sentence, most of this time he was treated as a 'trustee' and employed as a driver of the penitentiary carriages which allowed him outside the institution a lot of the time. He was released in February 1900.

In May of 1905, he shot up a bunk car that was parked on the Union Pacific Railroad near Byers, containing a crew of Greek laborers. Vorce objected to bringing foreign labor into Colorado. Two of the Greeks were injured. One man was crippled for life, and one lost a thumb. In November 1905, Vorce went into a Byers saloon and the owner Lon Smith got a gun on him, and assisted by others held him for the sheriff. (Because of the inaccuracies of newspaper accounts, it is thought this might have been Lon Sniff a well known Deer Trail saloon owner at that time). No record has been found of the sentence Vorce received for this offence. It was evidently county jail time, and one article said he was soon back in his old haunts.

To celebrate his release he went to LaSalle. Vorce made the station agent, Fred Norecross, dance while he fired his six shooter at the man's feet. The citizens threatened to send for the sheriff from Greeley. Vorce said, all right he'd wait. When the sheriff and a posse got there, Vorce was hiding behind a tree and got the drop on the sheriff and disarmed them all. He embarrassed them by parading them down the streets, following them with his guns pointing in their direction.

Vorce was once reported by a man from Golden for stopping him on the road and threatening to shoot him, because Vorce thought he was a deputy sheriff from Arapahoe County. Fortunately the man convinced him he was no deputy, and no injury occurred.

Vorce worked for Frank Cuykendall, near Roggen, for the last years of his life. Vorce married Nathilia (Ida) Duenweg Tomlinson, date unknown. His obituary said he married when he was eighty, which by this account would be around 1912. He died April 3, 1924 at the age of 92 in his home at 1966 Pearl Street. (*If that age is correct, that makes him born in 1832*). The funeral was held at Olinger chapel in Denver, and the body taken to Crown Hill for cremation.

1888 – Colorado State Penitentiary record says:

NO. 1714; NEWT VORCE; When convicted – **Apr. 20, 1888;** When received - **APR. 21,1888;** Crime – **MURDER;** County recvd. from – **WELD;** Age – **47;** Height – **5:10;** Complexion – **DARK;** Eyes – **BLUE;** Hair – **DR. BROWN, TURNING GRAY;** Occupation – **COWBOY;** Where born – **MARTINSBURG, VA;** Parents – **DEAD;** Married – **SINGLE;** Signature – **CAN'T WRITE;** Remarks – pretty long list of scars.
PARDONED BY GOV. JOHN L. ROUTT, JANUARY 1ST, 1893;

1893 – Colorado State Penitentiary record says:

NO. 3365; NEWT VORCE; When convicted – **NOV. 24, 1893;** When received – **NOV. 26,1893;** Crime – **ASSAULT TO MURDER;** Sentence - **10 YEARS;** County recvd. from – **WELD;** Age – **54;** Height – **5.91/2;** Complexion – **LIGHT;** Eyes – **BLUE;** Hair- - **GRAY;** Occupation – **RANCHMAN;** Where born – **VA.;** Parents – **DEAD;** Married – **NO;** (signed by warden); Signature – **CANNOT WRITE;** Remarks – very long list of scars.
DISCHARGED, FEB. 16, 1900

Resources: Rocky Mountain News, various issues; Greeley Tribune, Jan. 5, 1893, July 6 & 13, 1893, Nov. 11, 1893; Fort Collins Courier, Dec. 22, 1887, Apr. 26, 1888, July 20, 1893, Nov. 30, 1893; Denver Post, May 19, 1918; Fort Morgan Times, April 12, 1924; U.S. Army, 1865; Colorado State Penitentiary, U. S. Census

MOLLIE COLLIER

Friend and Aid to Newt Vorce

It is believed that Mollie Collier came to Deer Trail in about 1876. Unfortunately not much is known about her life until she became known for assisting the outlaw Newt Vorce. One Denver newspaper reported that "her people, believed to be wealthy and reputable, live in Wichita, Kansas." However, on a 1900 census, she gave her birth date as June 1860, but place of birth as "unknown."

When Newt Vorce escaped from the Arapahoe County jail in June of 1887, he was apparently aided by Mollie Collier. One story goes that he made his escape through a coal chute and that Mollie was waiting there, with a horse for Vorce. They made their get away to Deer Trail. There Vorce hid out at the Collier residence, where he had been living, off and on, for the past seven years.

The newspaper account of Mollie's residence is - "She lives in a hovel at Deer Trail, which is bare of furniture and contains only a suggestion of what poor people, hidden away in the alleys and by-ways of a big city, would have to shelter them. The house is old and dilapidated in construction, and the windows stuffed with paper and cloth, hardly sufficient to keep out the winds that have full sweep over the prairie."

For the next six months, Newt spent his nights at the Collier house, and would hide out somewhere in the area during the day. He even worked some, mostly odd jobs, during this time.

The main plan seemed to be to move around a lot, but he always returned to Mollie's at night. He was always prepared for an attack and the Collier house resembled a garrison every night. The windows and doors were barricaded to prevent a surprise. Vorce always slept with his clothes on and a gun under his pillow for his defense. Mollie and her daughter, Charity took turns standing watch.

Mrs. Collier was referred to as a grass widow who made her living taking in washing and serving as a cook. She was described by one newspaper as "a woman long past the time when a flush of young womanhood comes to the female cheek, coarse, and illiterate, and with the air that characterizes women of mining camps and variety shows, she has a brute-like devotion to the outlaw." Mollie had a daughter, who was thirteen years old at that time. The newspaper described her daughter as - "Mollie's ill-fed and scrawny child, who bears the appropriate name of Charity."

When the authorities arrived in Deer Trail in December, six months after the jail break, to take Vorce in, Mollie again aided Vorce by furnishing him with a horse. The first attempt failed. A search was made of her house and a horse with a "three circle bars" brand was found in back, bridled and saddled for use. The horse was confiscated and taken back to town to await being claimed by its owner. It is believed that she was successful later that night in taking a horse to where Newt was hiding outside of town. Vorce made his escape on the second horse, which was thought to have been Mollie's only horse and one of her few possessions of any value.

Mollie told a news reporter why Deputy Amos Cantley did not come after Vorce for six months, even though it was common knowledge that Vorce was in Deer Trail. She said Vorce and Cantley had been friends for many years. Mollie also knew Cantley very well, and knew his first wife, from whom he had only been divorced for a few weeks, her name was Alice Hagar. It seems Cantley was married to his second wife, Acie Payne, before this divorce took place. The first wife had returned to have him arrested for bigamy. Newt would have been an important witness for her case.

Mollie also stated that Newt's persecution was the result of his refusal to do some dirty work for the cattlemen. They wanted him to steal cattle from the poor settlers of 'poverty flats' and he refused. Mrs. Collier's story is corroborated in a few details by other people in the area.

Mollie Collier's devotion to helping Vorce was paid back when Sheriff Frank Hollingsworth, who was one of Vorce's chief pursuers, returned with a warrant for her arrest for hiding Vorce and assisting him in his escape. She was taken to Denver and held in the Arapahoe County jail.

Apparently Mollie was not in jail very long. It was said that the charges against her were never proven. Shortly after her release, Mollie moved to Byers, where she ran a boarding house. After operating her boarding house successfully for several years, she had accumulated a snug fortune. In 1896, she married a Mr. Roy, who was a questionable character, apparently after her property. Shortly after the marriage, her house burned down and Mr. Roy was indicted for arson. He jumped bail and was never seen again.

The lease for the ground on which the Roy hotel stood was destroyed in the fire. The railroad company, who owned the land tried to take possession of the land. Mrs. Roy succeeded in tying the matter up in the courts. In the mean time she erected another building and took up business again.

In 1898 charges were filed against George Holden, known as 'English George' for shooting up Mrs. Roy's house. The newspaper account said, "There are about four men in Byers who, when they tire of the company of any given party, begin firing guns and distributing lead in the immediate neighborhood of the obnoxious individual's home." When questioned, George said, "I heard some shooting but I didn't fire the shots. Shots are not such an unusual thing and I didn't look to see who was shooting." After deliberation, the Judge hearing the case announced that there was good reason to believe that 'English George' was the man who shot up the Roy place, and he was held over for trial.

Assistant District Attorney Haines said, "They seem to want to run Mrs. Roy out of Byers, but if they don't like her company they will have to leave themselves. Mrs. Roy is not the kind to be run out." The paper also stated that Mollie Roy can shoot like a mountaineer and ride the ugliest bronco that ever bucked. The hard talking Mrs. Roy is more prone to threaten than be threatened. She will not be run out of Byers for some time.

According to the 1900 census, she had gone back to using the name Collier, but was listed as married. Newt Vorce, who had been released from his second prison sentence in February of 1900, was listed as an employee of Mollie Collier.

Mollie's daughter Charity was arrested in 1896, at the age of 22, when she was running away with Joe Rico, a sheepherder whom she planned to marry. They were accused of stealing the three horses on which they made their escape. Charity said they would have gotten married in Byers but her mother would not have it.

They were accompanied by Julio Gonzales, also a sheepherder, and Mattie Roehling a fourteen year old friend of Charity's who was escaping abuse at home. Their immediate destination was Trinidad and then on to Mexico. They were apprehended near Ramah and Joe and Charity were taken to the Arapahoe County jail in Denver. Gonzales escaped when they were arrested and Mattie was sent to the State Industrial School for Girls in Denver.

The newspaper report describes Charity, "not what one would call a handsome or prepossessing girl. Poorly clad, with her coarse black hair disheveled about her head, swarthy complexion, large hands and feet."

Charity said they did not steal the horses. One of them belonged to Joe and the other two were loaned to them, and they intended to return them. Joe Rico and Charity Collier were arraigned in West Side Court on February 15, 1897, for horse stealing. A sympathetic and perhaps romantic jury acquitted the couple.

One year later, Charity happened to be back in Byers, visiting her mother at the time of the burning of Mollie's boarding house. Charity was married at that time, but not to Joe Rico, and living in southern Colorado near the state line.

Resources: Rocky Mountain News - various issues 1887, Dec. 13 & 14, 1896, Jan. 22, 1898, Aug. 21, 1898; Denver Post – Dec. 14, 1896, Feb. 15, 1897.

OTTO BROWN

Murder Mystery

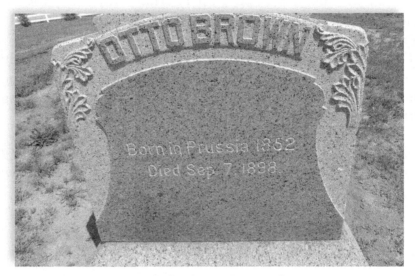

Headstone of Otto Brown, Evergreen Cemetery,
Deer Trail, Colorado.

here is a large light brown headstone sitting somewhat off by itself, on the north side, in section 4 of Evergreen Cemetery in Deer Trail. The stone reads "Otto Brown – Born in Prussia 1852 – Died September 7, 1898." This is the grave of a German immigrant whose birth name was in question. It was apparently thought to be Otto Goette, by some, and Otto Richter by others. He called himself Otto Brown. It's not known if he changed his name or just adopted Brown as his American name.

Otto Brown, as he was known, owned a sheep ranch located on Muddy Creek, about twenty-five miles north of Deer Trail. He kept to himself, and was known as a strong willed, cantankerous hermit who resented any visiting or trespassing on his land. He would shoot at the slightest provocation. Most of his neighbors avoided him or were afraid of him. He was known to have taken shots at anyone coming onto his property. He even had trouble keeping sheep herders. Many of them ran away scared, and some were run off by Brown at the point of a gun.

Is it any wonder Otto was missing for almost three weeks before anyone knew? Even after foul play was suspected, it was several more weeks before anyone was willing to go on his ranch to look for him, fearing that if he wasn't dead, he might show back up and start shooting.

The mystery began to unfold when Mr. Brown's sheep were sold in Omaha, Nebraska. Authorities discovered that the herd of about two thousand sheep was driven from Brown's ranch to Corona, about twenty-six miles north, by the man believed to have killed Otto. Corona was located about twelve miles west of Fort Morgan on the Burlington Northern Railroad.

Patrick Moore, a neighbor to the north of Brown, unknowingly met the stranger driving the sheep north in early September. Brown's brand was clearly visible on the sheep's backs. The stranger told Moore that they belonged to someone who had the same brand as Otto. Moore couldn't give a very good description of the man because the stranger had the lower part of his face covered with a handkerchief. He wore goggles and had his hat pulled down low.

Three days later the flock of sheep and the stranger arrived in Corona. The man gave his name as C. F. Newlin and consigned the sheep to be shipped by train to Omaha. He went along to see to the sale. Otto's wagon and two horses were later found abandoned four miles south of Corona. In the wagon was Otto Brown's nickel-plated, double action revolver. For many who knew Brown this was proof of his death. It was said that in order to take Otto Brown's beloved gun you would first have to kill him.

When Newlin arrived at the South Omaha stockyards, he sold the stolen flock for four thousand dollars. The manager of the stockyards evidently became suspicious, because he would only give Newlin fifty dollars in cash, placing the balance on deposit at the Colorado National Bank in Denver, where, if Newlin could be identified, he could claim his money. Newlin was soon on a train back to Denver where he was successful in withdrawing the money and immediately left town.

A group of men from Byers and Deer Trail set out to search for Otto, who was presumed dead at this point. Included in the search party were; C. S. Owens, G. A. Snow, Richard Price, John O'Connor, and Charles Cummings. When they arrived at Brown's ranch they found sixteen rams in the sheep pen and some distance away on the prairie they found several carcasses of rams which had been partly devoured by wolves. After a thorough search of the whole area, however, they found no sign of Otto.

The police later arrested Joseph Brewer, a Western Union employee, in Denver, for his part in helping to identify Newlin at the Bank. Brewer confessed that he gathered up enough 'reliable' people to say they knew Newlin, so that Newlin was able to claim the deposited money. Brewer was paid two hundred and fifty dollars for this service, but said he was guilty of no other wrong doing in the affair. He also told the police that Newlin's real name was Rush H. Beeler, but he knew nothing about his whereabouts after he left Denver.

Several Denver police detectives, going on tips and other evidence, made trips to Cheyenne, several locations in Nebraska, Salt Lake City, and San Francisco supposedly on the trail of Beeler, but never found any trace of him. It was slowly becoming a cold case.

Then in April of 1899, John Stark, nearest neighbor of the Otto Goette Brown ranch, discovered the remains of Mr. Brown less than half a mile from Brown's house. Stark was hunting along the Big Muddy Creek when his dogs stopped on the bank and after sniffing around, put up a dismal howl. Stark went to investigate and soon spotted a boot sticking out of the ground. On closer examination he could see the partially covered skeletal remains in the creek bank. The body had apparently been covered with soil until the spring flood had washed some of it away, exposing part of the body. Nearly eight months had passed since the disappearance and many people had been searching off and on since that time, probably riding right past that spot.

Stark assumed from the location of the body, that it was Otto Brown, but he had never seen Otto alive, because Stark had moved to the neighboring property after Otto's disappearance. Stark rode to get Otto's long time neighbor Lou Moore, and the two of them quickly returned to the scene. There was little to identify the body by except clothing remnants. "Yes, that is Otto Brown," said Moore the moment he saw the exposed leg, "I know it from that shoe, if nothing else. Brown always wore his shoes a couple sizes too big with the ends turned up."

They left the body undisturbed and Stark rode to Denver to summon the Coroner. Upon preliminary examination, a three inch indentation on the back of the skull, left no doubt that Otto had been murdered. His funeral was held at Deer Trail and Otto Goette, better known as Otto Brown, was buried there, in Evergreen Cemetery. He was forty-six years old.

Brown's sizable estate, said to amount to five thousand dollars, which was being handled by Public Administrator George Dimmit, undoubtedly paid for the large headstone. Mr. Dimmit also filed a claim, on behalf of the estate, against the company in Omaha that received Otto's sheep, but the company promised to go into bankruptcy if forced to pay the entire claim, and they settled in the amount of $3,200. Otto had no known relatives in this country, partly because no one knew him well enough to know anything about his background. A few people came forward claiming to be related, but none were able to show proof. The law at that time required the administrator to advertise for eight weeks for family to come forward, after that time the balance of the estate would be held by Arapahoe County until someone could prove a claim to it.

The police continued the search for R. H. Beeler. They were convinced that he had long ago left the state so they sent his description to police in many other states. The last known tip came six years later, in October of 1904, when Chicago police contacted Denver police saying that they had in custody a man fitting the description, who had been caught trying to sell a herd of sheep that had been stolen. Denver police sent them a photograph of Beeler for identification. Evidently this did not lead to a positive identification, nor apparently, was Beeler ever apprehended, because there is no coverage of it in the newspapers, and there is no record of Rush H. Beeler spending any time in the Colorado State Penitentiary.

In 1911, thirteen years later, two sisters, Melvina and Nona Richter came forward claiming Otto Brown was their uncle. They said that his real name was Otto Richter and he had disappeared from his large cattle ranch in Cheyenne, Wyoming, in 1894. He was said to be a man of silence and queer habits. About this time, a man fitting that description came to Byers and started a sheep ranch, changing his name to Otto Brown, the sisters claimed. At that time, authorities acknowledged that they had partial proof that Otto Brown was Otto Richter. No more information could be found to say if this claim was ultimately accepted.

Resources: Rocky Mt. News – Sept. 29, 1898, Sept. 30,1898, Oct. 1, 1898, Oct. 4, 1898, Oct. 5, 1898, Oct. 11, 1898, Apr. 25, 1899, Apr. 27,1899, Apr. 28, 1899, May 6,1899. Denver Post – Sept. 28, 1898, Sept. 30, 1898, Oct. 3, 1898, Oct. 5, 1898, Apr. 25, 1899, Apr. 28, 1899, Feb. 13, 1911. Aspen Daily Times: Nov. 4, 1904.

AGATE RANCHER GOES MISSING

Well Known Old Time Rancher

Nels Nelson ranks up at the top of the list of early day ranchers in eastern Colorado. Nels Christopherson Nelson was born in Norway in 1851. He came to the United States with his parents Christopher and Maren Nelson, and six brothers and sisters, in 1861. They settled in Minnesota where, as a boy, Nels made friends with the Indians and often hunted with them. He left home as a young man and headed west. Spending some time in Utah, eventually he came to Colorado where he was employed as a cowhand at the "Three Ring Ranch" owned by W. H. H. Cramner, three miles north of Agate.

When he was manager of the Cramner spread, in 1885, two horses were stolen from Cramner's stable one night. When Nelson missed them the next morning, he mounted up and started in hot pursuit. He rode hard on the trail of the horse thief. Finally arriving in Las Animas, he enlisted the help of Bent County Sheriff Frost. At midnight they spotted a campfire in the brush along the Purgatoire River. They were able to creep up on a man hovering over the small fire and get their guns on him. Nelson recognized the man as Joe Middleton, who was a notorious horse thief and trouble maker all over Colorado. Middleton offered no resistance. It took Nelson four days, but he got his man.

Nelson and Frost took Middleton to Trinidad then boarded a train to take him to Denver. At daybreak, as the train neared

Larkspur, Middleton somehow got out onto the platform and the next thing Nelson knew he saw Middleton rolling over and over on the ground, having jumped from the train. The train was moving about thirty miles per hour, so Nelson chose not to follow, rather he waited and got off at Larkspur and secured a horse and rode back down the track a couple of miles. He found Middleton lying on the ground, badly scratched, bruised and dazed, but with nothing broken. Nelson caught the next train to Denver with his prisoner in tow.

Nels married Polly Ann Thompson in 1877, they had two children and sadly, Polly died in 1885. Nels was so well known, that over a hundred cowboys from all over eastern Colorado came to her funeral. She is buried in the large tomb-like grave in the old part of Evergreen Cemetery in Deer Trail.

In the late 1880s, Nels Nelson purchased the Agate ranch from Cramner who had moved to Denver and was investing his fortune there. He also acquired the three ring brand, which had originally been John Hittson's Texas trail brand and was then passed to Cramner who was Hittson's son-in-law. Nelson's "V O V" brand also became well known.

Nelson married Cora S. Milland in 1887, and they had four children. Then trouble came in 1898, when Nels shot a man for being too friendly with his wife. Two different stories are told in the newspapers about this incident. The first says that Nelson came home unexpectedly one day and found twenty-six year old Gottlieb Egger visiting his wife. Egger left in a hurry but Nelson got off two shots, one hitting Egger in the shoulder as he fled.

The second newspaper story is what came out at the trial, so is probably a little more accurate. It says that Mrs. Nelson had driven to Deer Trail that day, and on the road, on her way home, she was met by Egger. Mrs. Nelson testified on the witness stand that Mr. Egger approached on horseback, and without invitation, seated himself beside her on the wagon and took unwarrantable liberties. This was witnessed by Mr. Nelson who happened to be riding in the vicinity. Nelson was armed with a rifle and shot Egger in the shoulder.

Which ever story is believed, soon after this incident, Nels divorced Cora. After spending two months in a Denver hospital recovering from his wound, Egger, who was also an Agate rancher, returned home and filed charges against Nelson for assault with intent to murder. The trial took place in May 1898. No record of the results of this trial could be found, but he must have had a sympathetic jury, because there is also no record of Nels Nelson spending any time in jail.

It seems everything took a turn for the worse for Nels after this. In November 1904, Nels took a trip to Kansas City to sell a train load of his cattle. He was accompanied by C. O. Howe, who reportedly held a mortgage on the cattle. Nelson received $4,000 for the herd. After returning to Denver, Nelson paid most of it to Mr. Howe. Nelson then rented a room at the Inter Ocean Hotel at Sixteenth and Blake streets in Denver, intending to return to Agate the next day. He was seen going out for a walk that evening about 11:30, and never returned. None of his friends or family ever saw or heard from him again. They were convinced that he had met with foul play. His possessions were left in his room, indicating he planned to return. Many people were aware that he had arrived in the city with a large sum of money. Most were probably not aware that he had already paid most of it out.

After a month of searching and investigating by the Denver police, they could find no trace of him, and no clues to follow. If he had been injured or killed during a robbery, as many feared, he would have turned up by that time. They began to believe that he had disappeared voluntarily. A news story on January 1, 1905, said police had traced Nelson to Portland, Oregon, but no other details. Also, during this investigation, it was discovered that Nelson's ranch, cattle, and all his possessions were heavily mortgaged.

In February 1905, some of the creditors went to court to ask for an injunction to stop the sale of cattle belonging to the missing Nelson. The herd, valued at about $5,000, was going to be sold in order to satisfy other claims against the estate, held by the Justice Court of Agate and the Elbert County sheriff. Additionally, Baldwin & Howe claimed to hold a chattel lien on the same herd. Creditors filing suite included, Richard Rico, John Jolly, and Clarence Brown. All sales of property were deferred pending a decision by the court. Ralph Smith was named as receiver.

The attorney representing the creditors stated that it was believed that Nelson was now in British Columbia. Where he got this information or why he believed this, is not known. However, by this time it seemed to be widely accepted that Nelson had gone to Canada, but nothing more was known. Even the family has very little information about what became of Nels. Information written by his granddaughter, Helen Schellenberg, says he married again in Canada and had two children, no names or dates. Some of the family believe that this perspective wife went with him to Canada when he disappeared. This information further states that Nels Nelson killed himself by gunshot in 1931. If this is true, it may have been on account of a terminal illness, he would have been eighty years old at that time.

Resources: Debbie Klausner; Rocky Mt. News - Feb. 28, 1885, May 21, 1898, Dec. 1, 1904, Dec. 5, 1904, Jan. 1, 1905, Feb. 25, 1905, May 18, 1905; Denver Post - May 7, 1898, May 20, 1898, Dec. 4, 1904, Dec. 11, 1904.

A MAD MURDERER

Respected Rancher Killed

At about six a.m. on the morning of October 14, 1884, a senseless and unprovoked murder took place. Mr. William P. Payne, a well liked sheep rancher, was shot and instantly killed at his home near Deer Trail, by Matt Perkinson, a sheep herder. There was no known trouble between the parties and no just cause for the crime.

The morning of the shooting, Will Payne, Mrs. Anna Sullivan the cook, and the hired man Jacob Miller, had just sat down to eat breakfast. Will's wife Acephine (Acie) was still in bed following the birth of their second son. The two children were also still sleeping. Matt Perkinson rode up, left his horse at the side of the house, and entered the kitchen door. Payne said, "Good morning Matt, won't you come eat breakfast with us?" Perkinson declined the invitation saying he couldn't stop because he had a bad acting horse. He went back toward the kitchen door and motioned for Payne to come outside. Will rose and followed him.

Some low conversation took place for a couple of minutes. Perkinson asked Payne if he could pay him the thirty dollars he owed him for his work last spring. Payne said he didn't have the money right then but would have it in a few days and would pay him. All of a sudden, Perkinson drew his gun and fired four shots. After the first shot hit Payne, he turned and tried to get back into the house, the next three shots hit Payne in the back. It all happened so quickly that by the time Jake Miller got up from the table and out the door, Payne was dead and Perkinson was riding away.

After carrying Mr. Payne's body into the house, Miller rode to Deer Trail to notify the sheriff. On his way to town he encountered Perkinson, who said he wanted to give himself up to Miller. Miller told him he wanted nothing to do with him and rode on into town. Perkinson arrived a short time later and gave himself up to Justice Hodge, who turned him over to Deputy Sheriff Stevens, who in turn took him to Denver to the Arapahoe County jail.

Matt Perkinson was from an upstanding family back east, and was a graduate of an Ivy League College. He became ill with tuberculosis and doctors advised him to come to Colorado for his health. Perkinson's father had known Acie Payne's father, Lauren Norton, in Topeka, Kansas, and knew that he had an interest in a ranch in Colorado and asked if the Payne's could give his son a job, which they did. Matt worked for Will Payne as a sheep herder for several years, with no trouble between them.

In the spring of 1884, while Perkinson and another herder were camped about eight miles from the home ranch, the other herder came home from Deer Trail late one night, intoxicated. The two of them got into an argument and the other herder shot Perkinson. When a neighbor rode by the next morning and noticed the sheep still in the corral, he went to see what was wrong. He found Perkinson shot and lying badly injured in his bunk. He got him to Deer Trail and they sent him to Denver on the train, where he spent several months in the hospital recovering.

When Perkinson was released from the hospital, he came back to Deer Trail and found work at the Pooler ranch, north of Deer Trail, dipping sheep. Other employees there later said that Perkinson acted strangely at times. On October 14th, he took a horse from Pooler's corral and rode to Will Payne's ranch.

"Mocking Bird Ranch" home, built by Will and
Acie Payne in 1880

Will Payne and his wife of two years, had come to the Deer Trail ranch from Topeka, Kansas in 1880. They named it "Mocking Bird Ranch," and built a fine two story frame house and started their family. Will had two sons at the time of his death, one was four and the other less than one month old. The ranch was on Middle Bijou Creek about three miles west of Deer Trail. The Paynes were well liked and active in the community, Will was Deer Trail postmaster at one time, and was appointed secretary of the school board in 1881.

After the shooting, feelings against Perkinson were strong in the area. Also there were rumors of an insanity plea which caused much anger. For that reason, his trial was moved to Elbert County. After many delays and postponements, a sanity hearing for Perkinson was finally held on May 27, 1886. By that time, Perkinson's condition had worsened to the point that even those who were outraged by the insanity plea had no doubt that Perkinson was insane. That was the verdict returned by the jury the next day. Perkinson was taken to the

Colorado State Mental Hospital in Pueblo where he died a year later.

It was thought that the isolation of the sheep camps for such long periods of time, coupled with being shot and left to die alone, might have deranged Perkinson. He may have then transferred his anger over the shooting to Will Payne, having no one else to take it out on. While in jail, he had also developed epilepsy and suffered frequent seizures, which were not understood at that time, and thought to be caused by a mental condition.

It has come to light in recent years, that during the first twenty years of existence of the State Mental Hospital, 1879-1899, that frequently patients who died there, and had no family to claim the body, were merely taken out on the grounds of the hospital and buried. Funding was very lacking for the hospital and the administration, during that time, did not have the money to cover the cost of burials. Many years later, as repairs and additions were made to the hospital, any excavation done on the grounds would unearth evidence of these graves. It is estimated that there may be as many as two hundred patients buried in unmarked graves on the grounds of the State Hospital. Anthropologists at Colorado State University are trying to locate and identify the remains.

Because Matt Perkinson died at the State Hospital in 1887, if his family from back east did not come forward and pay for his burial, he may have been one of those unfortunate souls.

Resources: "The Lauren Norton Family" by Constance Primus; Leadville Daily Herald Oct. 15, 1884, Oct. 16, 1884; Rocky Mt. News Oct. 15, 1884, May 28, 1886, May 29, 1886; Pueblo Chieftain – July 26, 1992; CSU news release – Oct. 23, 2006.

HUGO TRAIN ROBBERY

Passenger Murdered

O n Sunday night, August 5, 1900, a Union Pacific Train left Denver headed for Kansas City and points east. Just before 1:00 a.m. at a little spot named Lake, a few miles east of Limon, which consisted only of a coal chute and water tank, two men secretly boarded the train when it stopped for water. As soon as the train was moving again, the two men covered their faces with masks and pulled guns on the conductor and porter.

One bandit handed the conductor a flour sack and ordered him to hold it with both hands and walk ahead of him into the Pullman car and awaken the passengers one at a time. Once passengers were awakened, the bandit would tell them to be quiet or be killed, and demand they pass out all their valuables quickly. As the sleepy passengers did as they were told, all the loot was dropped into the sack.

When they finished in the first sleeper, they moved on to the second and continued their demands for money. As the masked men were about to rob Mrs. W. D. Harger of Denver, Mr. William J. Fay, a fellow passenger, in an apparent attempt to protect Mrs. Harger, pointed a revolver at the bandits through the curtain of his berth. It's not clear if Mr. Fay fired his gun or not, but almost immediately, one of the robbers shot Mr. Fay in the head, killing him instantly. They then fired four more shots as a warning to the other passengers, who were now very frightened.

One of the masked men told the conductor to pull the bell cord to stop the train. The conductor did so, but the train was moving very fast and did not immediately stop. The men told him to uncouple the car. The conductor explained he did not have the ability to do that. Finally just as they were nearing Hugo the train slowed, and stopped at Hugo. It is speculated that word may have reached the engineer about what was happening, and he may have delayed stopping until they reached a place where help was available.

William J. Fay was the former head of the Denver Gas Company. A few years earlier he had moved to California and was visiting Denver. He left his wife there while he traveled on to St. Louis on business. Fay's body was taken off the train at Hugo and put on a train back to Denver.

As soon as the train slowed enough, the criminals jumped from the train, forcing the conductor to jump first as a shield. Immediately, the two men ran off into the dark with their sack of loot. It was later estimated that they got about twenty-five dollars in cash plus some watches and jewelry. The conductor was released, and he returned to the train. It was believed that the robbers had someone bringing them horses or that they had horses stashed out somewhere for their escape. Within an hour, Sheriff John Freeman at Hugo had a posse in pursuit of the murders. They were soon joined by a dozen Pinkerton men out of Denver and Union Pacific Special Services from Omaha. They searched every mile around Hugo, but found no trail.

Acting on a tip from an informant, authorities arrested Marvin Sides and Frederick Merrick. These men were said to match the description of the two bandits, which was one tall man about six foot with sandy hair, and one much shorter about five foot six with dark hair. The tall man, doing all the talking had a heavy Texas drawl. The shorter man said nothing but he shot Fay.

Mark Sides who was arrested near Limon, owned a small ranch southwest of Agate and was married with two children. Besides owning a few cattle of his own, he often worked on the Jerome Matthews ranch. Mr. Matthews said he thought it highly unlikely that Sides had committed the crime. Fred Merrick, age 20, also lived and worked around Agate. He was arrested at the John Eggar ranch near Agate. Sides and Merrick were questioned by Union Pacific Special Services and released after a preliminary hearing at Hugo because there was no evidence against them.

Immediately after the robbery, orders were issued to all train crews on Colorado lines to be on the lookout for robbers. The crews were told to carry revolvers and use them if need be.

After almost a week, the detectives had about given up hope of catching the train robbers and murders because no clues of their whereabouts could be found. Finally, a break came when the two men were located hold up at a farm house near Goodland, Kansas. Apparently, they had been there since three days after the robbery.

They had first stopped at the home of Joseph Cullins, near Goodland, and asked for lodging. When they were refused, they became angry and threatening. Mr. Cullins threatened back with a shotgun, and the two strangers left. They next stopped at the home of D. E. Bartholomew, three and one-half miles northeast of Goodland, where they secured board and room for a few days.

Mr. Bartholomew stated later that the two men had been rather uncommunicative to the family, but had said their names were Howard and Gould. They were on their way to Nebraska, and they just needed to rest their horses for a few days. They claimed to be too tired to go into town, and paid Bartholomew's ten year old son to go to town each day and buy them a newspaper.

Mr. Bartholomew did not suspect the strangers or doubt their story. However, when a friend, Mrs. Dawson, visited the family, she thought the two men acted peculiar and communicated her suspicions to Sheriff Walker in Goodland. The following morning the sheriff recruited George Cullins and John Riggs to act as deputy sheriffs and made preparations to visit the Bartholomew farm.

News of the undertaking spread rapidly and a number of armed citizens joined the posse.

As a decoy, the sheriff and Cullins had dressed as cowboys and drove a bunch of horses to the farm. The Bartholomew family came out to greet them but not the outlaws. The other members of the posse closed in, and Sheriff Walker and John Riggs entered the house to arrest the men. When they went in and gave the order for the two occupants to put their hands up, the robbers drew their revolvers and a gun battle began. Two against two, they were exchanging shots as rapidly as possible. One bandit jumped out a window, the other went out the back door and ran. He was shot and killed by members of the posse who had surrounded the house. The remaining bandit ran back into the house for safety.

Two posse men were injured. John Riggs had been shot twice and seriously injured, George Cullins received one, less serious wound. They were taken to town for medical attention. Both men eventually recovered.

The remainder of the posse kept the other man pinned down in the house for several hours, exchanging fire occasionally. A member of the posse crawled through a corn field to reach the roof of a nearby shed; from there he was able to throw a lighted railroad fuse onto the roof of the house. Flames grew and soon enveloped the whole house, but the desperado never came out. He perished in the fire rather than surrender. Evidence of his remains was seen in the burning debris.

The two men's resistance to arrest had left no doubt that they were wanted criminals, and evidence found on the body of the dead man left no doubt that they were the train robbers. In his pockets were found bullets, two black face masks, a gold watch belonging to one of the train passengers, and a pocketbook containing several gold coins. Also on the body was a letter postmarked from Arroya, New Mexico, and addressed to Tiodora Arartano, Hugo, Colorado, it's unknown if this was a stolen item or a personal possession of the criminal.

The two dead train robbers were soon identified as James and Tom Jones, two Missouri and Texas desperadoes. Rewards of $3,000 in Missouri and $1,500 in Texas had been in place for a long time.

In addition to those rewards, the Union Pacific Railroad had put a $1,000 reward on both men following the Hugo robbery. Union Pacific immediately paid the rewards, and also paid $1,100 to Mr. Bartholomew whose home had been destroyed. They also covered the hospital bills of the two injured citizens, and several other bills contracted in the pursuit of the criminals, amounting to about $5,000 total.

A side note to this story, Mr. J. W. Olinger, well known Denver undertaker, was a passenger on this train. He was going east for his health. He was said to be in weak mental and physical health. His mental condition worsened rapidly after witnessing the robbery and murder, and he died soon after. His family blamed the train robbery for his death.

Resources: Aspen Democrat, Aug. 6, 1900, Aug. 9, 1900, Aug. 10, 1900, Aug. 11, 1900, Aug. 12, 1900; Rocky Mountain News, Aug. 9, 1900; Elbert County Banner, Aug. 10, 1900; Yuma Pioneer, Aug. 10, 1900; Akron Weekly Pioneer, Aug. 10, 1900; Summit County Journal, Aug. 11, 1900, Sept. 1, 1900; Aspen Daily Times, Aug. 11, 1900; Durango Democrat, Aug. 11, 1900; Aspen Tribune, Aug. 12, 1900; Carbondale Chronicle, Aug. 13, 1900, Aug. 20, 1900; Colorado Transcript, Aug. 15, 1900; "Case Files of Leonard DeLue, Pinkerton Man"

REVENGE OR JUSTICE

Murderer – Rapest Burned at the Stake

All Colorado newspapers in November, 1900 were using the
terms, "brutal murder," "atrocious crime," "fiendish killing," to describe the rape and murder of a thirteen year
old girl near Limon.

Louise Frost lived with her parents on a sheep ranch about
a mile and a half from Limon. On November 8th, she failed to
return home from school at the regular time. Her father, Robert
Frost became uneasy and started down the road to meet her.
Before he had gone far, he found the horse and empty cart Louise
had taken to school. The alarm was spread quickly and friends and
neighbors began searching for Louise.

Louise's mutilated body was soon found in a draw about fifty
feet off the road only a half mile out of Limon. She was still alive
when found, but unconscious and she died shortly after being tak-
en to her home, never regaining consciousness.

The search party searched until dark for any traces of the killer,
with no success. The next morning bloodhounds were sent from
Colorado Springs, but because of a frost during the night, the
scent was lost. A bloody handkerchief was found near the scene.
When it was shown around, it was recognized as belonging to John
Porter, a black youth who had been working in the area for several
months. He and his father and brother had come to Limon from
Kansas, where both John and his brother had recently been released from a reformatory after serving time for assault on a young

102

woman. When Lincoln County Sheriff Freeman went to question Porter, he was nowhere to be found. An alert was sent out to law officers along the Union Pacific line, thinking he probably escaped by train.

A few days later, John Preston Porter was arrested in Denver for suspicion of murder. Sheriff Freeman went to Denver to question the suspect. Freeman took with him the handkerchief and also a pair of boots that had been found near Porter's bunk house. The boots were badly charred as if someone had tried to burn them up. The soles of the boots matched prints found at the scene. Porter admitted both items belonged to him.

Confronted with this evidence and after many hours of questioning, John Porter calmly confessed to the horrible deed. Porter said he left work at noon, and went to a place by the side of the road where he knew the girl would pass by. He waited there, out of sight. When asked if he had known Louise Frost, Porter answered that he had seen her often around the school house but never spoken to her. When the horse got within hearing, Porter hollered for it to stop, and it did. Porter told the girl to get out of the cart, and she did. Then he took her by the neck into the bushes and assaulted her. He then took his knife and stabbed and cut her and then stomped on her head when she didn't seem to die. Porter said he killed her because he was afraid she would tell.

As soon as Robert Frost and others in Lincoln County heard that Porter had confessed and there was no doubt that he was the killer, they began calling for justice suitable to the horrific crime. Soon a vigilante group formed and began plans for the execution of John Porter.

The death penalty, which had been law in Colorado since 1859, was abolished by courts and politicians in 1897. Since that time, the citizens had watched case after case as murders were put in jail for a few years, and were soon back on the streets as free men. This had people upset and disappointed at the justice system. That, coupled with the brutality of this premeditated murder and the age of the innocent victim, had people out for revenge. They knew 'just punishment' would not happen if left to the government officials.

On November 16th, Porter was turned over to Sheriff Freeman in Denver. Freeman would take Porter, by train, to the Lincoln County jail in Hugo. By this time the rumors of the vigilantes' plans to hang Porter had circulated everywhere. When the sheriff boarded the train with Porter, it was crowded with newspaper correspondents and curiosity seekers. At every station and watering tank along the route, people were gathered, and roars of anger would greet the train as it passed.

The train arrived in Limon at 3:45 p.m. When the train stopped, it was boarded by sixteen armed men, who had been appointed for this duty. They demanded the sheriff turn the prisoner over to them. The sheriff protested in the name of the law and said the prisoner would be taken to Hugo and held for trial. Despite all the sheriff's efforts, a noose was placed around Porter's neck and he was removed from the train.

At the station, they were greeted by three hundred armed men along with two hundred citizens, including women and children, who had known and loved Louise Frost. Robert Frost, the father of the victim, expressed that hanging was too easy payment for what his daughter had suffered. The vigilante group decided to leave the method of death to the victim's father. He decided upon burning at the stake.

Porter was taken to the scene of the crime, where the body of Louise was found. The huge crowd followed. A railroad rail was used as a stake. Hay, sage brush, and wood were hauled to the scene. Preparations for the execution took about two hours. During this time, Porter sat calmly and read from a Bible that he'd been given in jail. As the time came near, Porter tore pages from the Bible and handed them out to people in the crowd for souvenirs. Porter was bound to the stake with ropes and chains. The father of Louise set the match to the oil soaked combustibles.

In the end, most of the vigilantes could not abide the agony caused by this method of execution. One newspaper reported that at the first scream from Porter, about five hundred shots were fired into the fire to end his suffering.

John Porter's father threatened to sue the State of Colorado. Many threats of charges were made against Sheriff Freeman for failure to protect his prisoner, and against Robert Frost and the citizens who took part in the execution. But nothing ever came of these threats and no arrests were ever made.

Sheriff Freeman made a statement saying, in part, "Under the current laws of this state neither rape nor murder is punishable by death, nor are rape and murder combined punishable by death. Yet every man of common sense knows, who is at all familiar with the horrible particulars of the rape of Louise Frost, and her fiendish murder, that the citizens of Lincoln County would not wait for the slow process of the law and the wholly inadequate punishment that would come as the result of a conviction under the law."

All of the lawyers and politicians, who were making the threats, deep down knew how they would feel about it if this had been their daughter. They also realized what they would have done in the sheriff's place, if confronted by three hundred armed men. They also knew what the result would be when these cases came before juries made up of citizens who felt the same way as those accused. Because of this case and other vigilante executions in the state, the death penalty was reinstated in the State of Colorado in 1901.

Resources: Wray Rattler, Nov. 17, 1900; Silver Cliff Rustler, Nov. 21, 1900; Durango Democrat, Nov, 17, 1900; Aspen Daily Times, Nov. 17, 1900, Nov. 25, 1900; Pagosa Springs News, Nov. 30, 1900; Summit County Journal, Nov. 17, 1900.

HARRY POTTS MURDER

Killed For His Bank Roll

The body of Harry Potts was found in a well on his property in Elbert County on May 13, 1907. Mr. Potts' head had been crushed in two places. His body had been dumped into the well and covered with dirt, only his limbs were partially exposed, which led to the discovery of the body.

Harry Potts was a widower, in his late sixties. He lived alone on his small place in the east end of Elbert County on Wilson Creek northeast of Agate, near the W ranch. He lost a leg in the Civil War and walked with the help of a wooden stump, as was the custom of the day. Potts had not been seen since he was in Deer Trail on April 24th, which prompted the search of his property.

Coroner Evans of Elizabeth was sent for, upon the discovery of the crime, and preliminary findings were that Potts was murdered by two blows to the head, apparently by a hammer. Sheriff Maguire immediately began investigating the crime and tracking down the killer. This was also the first murder case for a young Roy Brown, who was sheriff of Elbert County for the next thirty years.

Witnesses in Deer Trail said that Mr. Potts had about $300 on his person when he left for home on the evening of April 24th. There was no cash found on his body or anywhere on his property when he was found. This established robbery as the motive for the murder.

Potts left Deer Trail in the company of Sylvester Craig, a young man who did nothing in particular, and who always seemed to be broke and looking for work. Craig had befriended Potts earlier that day and it was presumed that Potts may have hired Craig to do some work for him. Witnesses also added that this same young man was seen back in Deer Trail on April 25th, with plenty of money, and said he was headed to Texas. He was seen buying a ticket to Denver where he outfitted himself with new clothes and bought a ticket to Topeka, Kansas. From Topeka he went to Dallas where he was apprehended.

The newspaper reported that Sheriff Maguire left for Dallas, Texas, on May 24, 1907 to bring back Sylvester Craig, the suspected killer of Potts. Craig was held in jail in Denver until his trial, because of the strong feeling against him in Agate and Deer Trail.

Not much is known about Sylvester Craig, except that he originally came from Topeka, Kansas. Craig was nineteen years old at the time he was arrested and charged with murder. Craig was tried in Elbert County District Court on July 26, 1907. This trial resulted in a hung jury, the vote being eight for conviction and four for acquittal. A second trial was scheduled for November.

The November trial resulted in a guilty verdict. Craig was sentenced by Judge Morris to ninety-nine years in the penitentiary. He was taken to the Colorado State Penitentiary in Canon City where he became prisoner number 6940.

Harry Potts may have been buried on his property, because one newspaper said he was buried at Agate. Potts had two grown daughters living in Rocky Ford.

On December 14, 1917, for some reason, five murders who had been sentenced to spend the rest of their lives in the penitentiary were selected and granted commutations of their sentences by the state board of pardons. Sylvester Craig was one of those lucky inmates. After serving ten years of his life sentence, his sentence was commuted to twenty-five years. However, the prisoners had to, first, by good behavior and work in the road camps, make themselves eligible for parole. Sylvester Craig did this and was released on parole July 5, 1921, at the age of thirty-three.

In February 1918, a nine and ten year old boy and girl fell through the ice on a reservoir near Canon City. All available agencies were sent for. The prison warden hurried a dozen trustees to the scene to assist in the rescue. Sylvester Craig and another prisoner, Jimmy Stanton, brought the two children to the surface after plunging into the icy water with ropes tied around their waists. Unfortunately, Doctors at the scene were unable to revive the children. This may have earned Craig a few points toward his early release.

Resources: Elbert County Banner - May 17, 1907, May 24, 1907, July 26, 1907, Nov. 15, 1907; Rocky Mt. News - May 17, 1907, May 19, 1907, Dec. 15, 1917; Denver Post – May 17, 1907, May 18, 1907, Dec. 15, 1917; Pueblo Chieftan – Feb. 18, 1918; Colorado Springs Gazette – July 25, 1907; Colorado State Penitentiary.

HERMAN BANDY

A Cunning Killer

Herman Henry Bandy,
early 1900s

Herman Henry Bandy was a good-looking man, charming, polite, friendly, and very likable. But these were merely tools of his trade and he used them very well. He probably came by his dishonesty from his father, Jabel Bandy. When Herman was young, the family, his Mom, Dad, and six sisters, moved around a lot. When they moved to a new town, Jabel would immediately join a church and even volunteer to teach Sunday school. After awhile he'd stay home occasionally, and send the wife and kids to church. He would go to the homes and farms of the neighbors whom he knew to be at church and help himself to whatever food, supplies, or valuables he found. Jabel fed his family by stealing food and butchering other people's livestock, etc. Being raised in this manner, Herman learned to take whatever someone had that he wanted and by whatever means necessary.

Herman was born in 1885, and while living in Missouri, in 1904, he entered a marriage arranged by his father and the father of Lucinda Eldringhoff. Following the wedding they moved to Gage, Oklahoma, where Lucinda's brother John was living. John was married to Herman's sister Olive Bandy. Around 1907, Herman and 'Sindy' moved to Elbert County, Colorado, where Herman's sister Stella and her husband Sam Yoder were living. Also, Sindy's sister Cecilia and Al Nelson soon homesteaded nearby.

Setting the pattern for the rest of their married life, besides moving around a lot, Herman would not work, so Sindy got a job as a housekeeper at the Guy Morrow ranch for $.50 a week.

Herman took up a homestead in the Pines, southwest of Deer Trail, and built a one room log house to accommodate his growing family. Ultimately, he failed to prove up on this homestead. Herman was often away for long periods of time, and Sindy had no idea where. He would say he was working or looking for work, but he never returned with any money. During this time Sindy became aware of his dishonesty. No one will probably ever know how many crimes he committed. Over time, details of a few have surfaced.

One evening in January of 1910, Herman told Sindy that he was going to run over to his good friend and neighbor's place to see if he wanted to travel with him to Byers the next day for supplies. Bandy had befriended P. T. Ochs, who lived alone on his nearby homestead, and they spent a lot of time together. The next morning Mr. Ochs did not show up for their scheduled trip to town and Herman decided to go check on him. When he arrived at Ochs' place he found Ochs dead. Apparently he had shot himself in the head. The newspaper reported Ochs was upset about his son being arrested on Federal Mail Fraud charges. This story was probably provided to the press and police, along with the suicide theory, by Herman Bandy. Ochs left a wife and five children.

In 1911, Bandy had spent some time in Cheyenne, Wyoming, for what purpose no one knew. In June, authorities brought him back to Elbert County to answer to charges of horse stealing. Bandy was in possession of horses and a wagon belonging to Ernest Moore of Cheyenne. Moore had reportedly been killed by accident while he and Bandy were shooting prairie dogs the previous week. Moore was putting his rifle behind the seat when it caught on something and discharged, shooting Moore in the head. Bandy was the only witness. Apparently Bandy had something that showed that he had purchased the team and wagon from Moore in Cheyenne, charges against him were dropped. Moore left a wife and six boys under the age of nine.

In 1913, Bandy befriended a young couple named Franklin who were staying in the cabin with the Bandy's, apparently until they could build a place of their own. One March morning, young Albert Franklin and Herman Bandy set out in team and wagon to go to Deer Trail for supplies. They stopped at a spring along the way and saw a hawk circling overhead. Bandy got his shotgun and got off the wagon and bet Franklin that he could bring it down. As he was shooting around in the air at the hawk, he accidently hit Al Franklin, the shot entering under his chin and exiting the top of his head. As Bandy told this story to the authorities, he was in tears because of accidently shooting "the best friend he ever had."

*Grave of Albert T. Franklin 1877-1913, located in Bijou Basin
along Road 150. He was buried beside the Bijou Baptist
Church, which was later moved a few miles east to
Road 101. Now his grave sits alone on the prairie.*

Three days later, the Elbert County Sheriff in Kiowa received an anonymous message by telephone to the effect that if H. H. Bandy was not locked up or taken away, he would be dealt with severely. Because many friends and neighbors did not believe the 'accidental' shooting of Franklin was an accident. The sheriff, with several deputies, went to the Bandy place to take Bandy to Kiowa for his own protection. Bandy did not want to go and told the deputies that his brother-in-law, Al Nelson, who was known as a crack shot, would not stand by and let them take him in. Finally, the sheriff was able to persuade Bandy that it would be foolish to stay at his homestead alone if trouble would start. He accompanied them to Kiowa where he was kept for a few days to let the trouble die down.

After he was released, Herman came home and told Sindy to pack, because they were leaving Colorado, giving no explanation. They quickly loaded what possessions they could onto a wagon, along with Sindy and three children, and left that night. Sindy knew Bandy must have been in serious trouble because they continued to travel at night and camp in wooded areas. He stole grain and milk from farms along the way. They ended up back in Gage, Oklahoma.

The Bandy family continued to move around in Oklahoma and then back to White Church, Missouri, where Sindy's family lived. Little is known of Bandy's exploits during this time except petty theft from neighbors. Sindy and the children survived by selling milk and eggs, which the children delivered in their little red wagon. One day Herman came home riding a fine horse and leading another and said he was delivering them to someone, and went on his way. The next day the authorities came by looking for Bandy and the stolen horses. Apparently he was enough ahead of them and he escaped capture again.

In 1925, the family, now consisting of seven children, moved back to Gage, Oklahoma. Bandy's story was that he had leased a farm from Pete Milesi, paying him $500. The sixty-seven year old Milesi planned to return to Germany. Bandy claimed that Pete kept putting him off about taking possession of the farm. One day Bandy went to confront Pete about it and Pete was shot in the head and killed. After stealing Pete's watch and money, Bandy hid the body in a straw stack. Apparently Bandy's plan was to burn the straw stack to destroy the evidence and tell everyone that Milesi had indeed gone back to Germany, leaving Bandy the farm.

Bandy told his wife that he and Pete were gambling and Pete pulled a gun on him and he had to shoot him in self defense. Sindy did not believe his story, she had heard too many similar stories in the past and knew it had to stop. She and the seven children walked to the nearest neighbors who took them to Sindy's brother's home where she called the police and reported the killing. The police found the body in the straw stack and arrested Bandy. His story to the police was that he had made arrangements to buy Milesi's place for $3500. When he went to Milesi's place that day, Pete accused him of informing the authorities about the liquor still Pete was operating in his house. Bandy said Pete went and got a gun and he had to shoot Pete in self defense. When asked why he had carried his .22 rifle into Pete's house when he just went to talk business, Bandy said he had a dog in his truck and was afraid he would knock the gun off the seat and damage it. When the police searched Pete's house the only weapon they found was a .32 caliber revolver in a desk drawer in another room.

Bandy was tried and found guilty of murder. He was sentenced to life in prison and sent to McAllester Oklahoma State Prison on April 15, 1926. He used his charm and good behavior and soon became a trustee. He used that privilege to escape on July 7, 1928. He was never apprehended.

Bandy had threatened Sindy for turning him in to the police. She was probably uneasy the rest of her life, but as far as anyone knows, she received only one letter from him after his escape and never heard from him again. Bandy visited Sindy's sister, Cecilia, where they had lived at Deer Trail, Colorado, a couple of times. Also, several years later, Sindy's brother-in-law, Alvin Riggs, who lived in Harrison, Arkansas, recognized Bandy on the street one day. The next day they heard there had been a murder in that part of town the previous night.

Resources: Elbert County Banner, Jan. 21, 1910, Jan. 23, 1911; Summit County Journal, June 17, 1911; Colorado Transcript, Mar. 6, 1913; San Juan Prospector, Mar. 8, 1913; Denver Post Mar. 4, 1913; Rocky Mt. News, Mar. 6, 1913; Colorado Springs Gazette, Mar. 5, 1913; Ellis County Capitol, Jan. 15, 1926.

BULLY – BULLY PARADE

Cowboys Honor President

In 1910, the year after Theodore "Teddy" Roosevelt left office as the President of the United States, he came to Denver for a visit. This was a big event for Colorado cowboys, because Teddy was not only the former president, and by some, considered the greatest man on earth, but he was one of them, an ordinary down to earth cowboy.

Teddy was to arrive in Denver on August 29th. There would be a parade that morning upon his arrival. The Denver Press Club had arranged that following the parade, he would be escorted to Overland Park for a chuck wagon dinner, to be prepared under the supervision of Louis Callahan of Deer Trail.

Callahan was renowned as an exceptionally good chuck wagon cook. He was considered a landmark around Deer Trail, because he'd been there so long. He was a former Negro slave who came to Deer Trail as a cook with John Hittson's cattle drives in the late 1860s. He stayed on and cooked for Hittson's round-ups for many years. Callahan married and took up a homestead on Middle Bijou Creek in 1888. He was still in demand as a cook at round-up time. By 1910, however, he had retired from cooking, but for Teddy Roosevelt he made an exception.

A big blow out was planned and word was spread to all the cowboys in the country. On August 27th, they all gathered in Deer Trail. All anyone needed to join the party was a good horse and a bedroll. Some of the names in the group were – Maher, Thayer,

Price, Crandall, Deter, Scherrer, Jolly, and Jim Scott, who rode a beautiful white gelding that he was really proud of. Jim Scott was the organizer of the Deer Trail cowboys, and also furnished one of the chuck wagons. They were joined by groups of cowboys from Agate, the pines, and most of eastern Colorado.

After the hurrahing was over that evening, they camped in the cottonwoods along East Bijou Creek that night. Early the next morning they saddled up and escorted Callahan and the chuck wagon to Denver. They were joined by more cowboys as they rode along. When they camped near Union station that night, they were one hundred and fifty strong.

They were up early the morning of the parade. Horses were brushed and groomed and gear was polished until it shown. They all dressed in their best duds. The group assembled on Wazee Street and rode to Seventeenth and Blake where the parade was forming.

Cowboys riding in the parade down Seventeenth
Street in Denver to honor Teddy Roosevelt,
August 29, 1910.

116

A military escort was waiting to greet Mr. Roosevelt with a twenty-one gun salute, when he arrived at Union Station. The procession then moved up Seventeenth Street as the troops saluted and the band played "Hail Columbia." The parade began at 11:00 a.m. as Teddy took his place at the front. Following the former president, Governor Shafroth, and Mayor Speer, and many other dignitaries, was a large congregation of United Spanish War veterans and a few old Civil War veterans. The two mile long parade had 5,000 participants, and 1,500 were mounted rough riders or cowboys.

The Deer Trail area cowboys were right in the midst of the line-up and a lot of the boys were showing off with their horses and ropes. The crowd loved it. It was the largest parade Denver had ever had up to that date, and the crowd, estimated at 250,000 the largest to witness a parade. The entire city was dressed in patriotic attire and waving flags. Hundreds of people rented hotel rooms that faced the parade route, for the day, to have a comfortable view of the parade.

Former President Theodore Roosevelt waving to the crowds of people, lining Seventeenth Street and watching from the windows. Denver, 1910.

117

Teddy's open car stopped in front of the Brown Place Hotel, and he watched the parade pass in review. After the parade, Teddy changed into his cowboy gear and was escorted down Broadway to Overland Park, where the big feed was to take place. Callahan and his crew had been there preparing the steak dinner since very early that morning. The cowboys, the press, and the Colorado Sheriffs were the only others invited to the feast, and arrived shortly after the president.

Just as the eastern plains cowboys arrived at the park, Jim Scott's prized white horse suddenly dropped dead. They thought it must have been a heart attack from too much heat and excitement. Everyone had to razz Jim about what kind of a horse his pride and joy turned out to be, and Jim took it pretty good, but really everyone felt bad for him.

There were two chuck wagons, the one furnished by Jim Scott and one by Charlie Gant of Ft. Collins. The area around the cookfires had been roped off. Roosevelt was served the first steak and pronounced it "Bully Bully good." The rest of the huge crowd was then fed.

Teddy circulated amongst the cowboys and shook hands and called some of them by their first names. He always possessed a great memory for names. One of the cowboys who was there, later remarked, "What a great thrill it was getting close to such a great man who actually enjoyed mingling with plain old ranch hands."

Resources: Bully, Bully Parade by Agnes Puga; Steamboat Pilot, Aug. 31,1910; Rocky Mountain News – Aug. 28, 1910; Denver Post – Aug. 28, 1910, Aug. 29, 1910; Denver Public Library

FEUD ENDS IN DEATH

Stewart Lanterman killed

Alongstanding feud between two neighbors ended with a gun battle that left one man dead. Many rumors were circulated regarding the cause of the bad feelings between the two men who lived only three miles apart.

On October 16, 1912 a construction crew was building a bridge across Beaver Creek about twenty-five miles northeast of Deer Trail, forty-five miles south of Fort Morgan, in the southern part of Washington County. Stewart Lanterman was one of the workmen. At about five p.m. they were preparing to quit for the day. Lanterman was beginning to hitch up his buggy for the trip home.

A wagon with two men pulled up. One of the men was George Terry, the sworn enemy of Lanterman. It's not known if his appearance on the scene was accidental, as Terry later claimed, or if it was planned on his part.

When Terry saw Lanterman he yelled, "Is it true you said you would shoot me on sight?" When he received no reply from Lanterman he fired two shots. Lanterman ran to his buggy and retrieved his .22 caliber long rifle and more shots were exchanged. Then Lanterman started to run for better cover, and at least one of Terry's next three shots hit Lanterman. Lanterman fell, mortally wounded, but he supported himself up on one elbow and continued firing at Terry a few more times, but his shots went wild. Terry approached Lanterman where he had fallen and deliberately shot him in the head.

When Terry saw that Lanterman was dead, he rode to Deer Trail and gave himself up to Deputy Sheriff Albert Reed. Terry claimed self defense. Reed took the prisoner to Akron the next day to turn him over to Washington County authorities, because the crime had occurred across the line into Washington County.

There were ten eye witnesses to the killing. Nine members of the construction crew watched the whole thing and were powerless to do anything to stop it. The tenth witness was William J. Fleming who drove the wagon in which Terry arrived. Fleming was later charged as an accessory, supposedly dealing with the fact that Terry's arrival was not accidental. Terry claimed he had been out looking for his horses for several days. When he met Fleming, he asked to ride along with him on the wagon to continue looking for the horses.

The stories of what the feud was about were many, but they became more numerous and more colorful after the killing. One rumor was that it began over range rights and fence issues. Another was that Blain Lanterman, Stewart's brother, had accused George Terry of being friendly with his wife, threats were made, and Stewart took up this fight. Enough harsh words and threats were exchanged between Stewart and George Terry that it became a personal grudge.

The trial of George Terry for first degree murder, started on January 27, 1913, in District Court at Akron. Terry's defense stated that at a dance at the Simpson school house, which George Terry, Blain Lanterman and his wife all attended, Lanterman's wife had flirted with George Terry. Of course, Lanterman's account of this incident had Terry doing the flirting. Terry also stated that later, Mrs. Blain Lanterman came to Terry's home and asked him to give her three hundred dollars. The reason was not given, but it could have been so that this incident would not be discussed with Terry's wife.

Terry stated, when he refused to pay the money, Blain took up his wife's cause and threatened to poison Terry's stock and kill his dog, if he didn't come up with the three hundred dollars. Terry claimed these threats continued for two years, then, just forty-eight hours before the shooting, George Terry heard the rumor that Stewart Lanterman had threatened to shoot him on sight. George's defense was that he heard these stories and believed them, and acted on them, rather than wait to be ambushed by Lanterman.

Before the completion of the trial, George Terry made a deal and pled guilty to second degree murder. The Judge sentenced him to not less than nineteen and not more than twenty years in prison. After being held over to testify in the case of Will Fleming, he was taken to Colorado State Penitentiary in Canon City where he became prisoner number 8678, in February 1913. Terry was forty-six years old, married, and listed his address as Simpson, Colorado. After only seven years, he was pardoned in May 1920, but for some reason was not released until November 1920.

Resources: Akron Weekly Pioneer - Oct. 18, 1912, Dec. 27, 1912, Jan. 31, 1913; Yuma Pioneer - Feb. 7, 1913; Rocky Mt. News - Oct. 18, 1912, Jan. 27, 1913; Denver Post – Jan. 27, 1913, Jan. 30, 1913; Colorado State Penitentiary.

DEER TRAIL BANKS ROBBED

Two For One

Deer Trail State Bank, at First and Elm, shortly
after it was built in 1910

In the early morning hours, somewhere between the time the new electric street lights were extinguished at midnight, and before dawn, of October 12, 1920, bank robbers broke into both banks in Deer Trail, cleaned out the cash and made their escape undetected. By the time the robberies were discovered when the banks opened at 8:00 the next morning, the wealthy robbers were long gone.

The burglars entered into the basement of the Deer Trail State Bank through a coal chute. One Denver newspaper reported that they cut through the floor to enter the bank. The Deer Trail Tribune said they used the stairs and broke in the stairway door. The combination lock was blown off the safe with a small charge of nitroglycerin. Losses were estimated at three to four thousand dollars. All the safety deposit boxes were smashed and all cash and bonds were taken from them. The loss there was unknown, but could have amounted to thousands of dollars. The Deer Trail State Bank sold $100,000 worth of Liberty and Victory bonds during the war, (World War I). It was feared that a large portion of these were locked up in these boxes.

The bold band of thieves then moved to the other end of the block and broke into the First National Bank of Deer Trail by breaking a lock on the back door. Again, the lock on the safe was blasted open. Then it seems the robbers work was interrupted by some scare, because they fled the bank without gaining entry into the vault. They overlooked $1,200 left in the cashier's cage.

The car that the robbers used was parked on the main street, with the engine running, and lights dimmed, during the robberies, within one hundred feet of the home of Mrs. Carley Jolly. Mrs. Jolly was expecting her husband home about that time. Seeing the car, and assuming it was her husband, she opened a window and called to him. She got no reply, and a short time later, three men came and got in the car and they leisurely drove away. This was not reported by Mrs. Jolly until the next day when she heard about the robbery.

Cashier Ralph Tilton of the Deer Trail State Bank entered the bank the next morning to open the bank for business and discovered the destruction and the ransacked vault. Police were notified right away, but the thieves were miles away by that time.

The robbers left behind a flashlight and a number of candles at the First National Bank, but no other clues. Residents of Deer Trail said they had seen a large automobile driving around town the previous evening. The car contained four strangers, three men and one woman. Many witnesses, however, were not sure one of the passengers was a woman.

Before entering the banks, the bandits had cut all the telephone wires leading out of town, but for some reason overlooked the telegraph wires. It was later discovered that a painter's ladder was stolen from the fairgrounds to accomplish this task.

A long, hard investigation of the double break-in went nowhere. A five hundred dollar reward was offered by the United States Fidelity and Guaranty Company for the conviction of the burglars, but no one was ever arrested for these crimes.

Many years later (about 1975), Claude Stanush wrote about the Newton Boys in a Life Magazine article. He later wrote a book on the same subject. The book was made into a movie in 1998. In the Life magazine article, Willis Newton, leader of the gang, told Stanush a list of a few of the banks his gang had robbed. On the list was Deer Trail, Colorado in the amount of six thousand dollars.

The Newton Boys were four brothers from Uvalde County, Texas: Willis, Doc, Joe, and Jess. From 1919 to 1924, they robbed eighty-seven banks and six trains, from Texas to Canada. They were not as famous as Bonnie and Clyde and others, because they didn't rob banks at the point of a gun, and they never killed anyone. Their robberies were mostly done by breaking into the banks at night.

The brothers were wanted in almost every state west of the Mississippi. Eventually they were all caught and prosecuted for one crime or another and all spent various sentences in prison. After they were released, many years later, they returned to Texas and most of them managed to stay out of trouble for the most part. Three of them lived to be in their eighties and nineties.

When Joe Newton, the youngest brother was seventy-nine, in 1980, he was interviewed by Johnny Carson on the Tonight Show. He told Johnny that the Newton's were blamed for every bank that was robbed during those years, most of which they didn't do, but they also robbed a lot of banks that no one ever knew about. He also said that they knew Bonnie and Clyde, but didn't approve of them because they robbed filling stations and shot too many people. Joe was the last of the brothers to die in 1989, at the age of eighty-eight.

I think there is enough coincidence here to find them guilty of the double robbery in Deer Trail in 1920. An unsolved mystery solved?

Resources: Fort Collins Courier, Oct. 12, 1920; Littleton Independent, Oct. 15, 1920; Life Magazine (date unknown); Denver Post, Oct. 12, 1920, Oct. 17, 1920; Rocky Mountain News – Oct. 14, 1920; Deer Trail Tribune, Oct. 16, 1920, Oct. 20, 1920, Wikipedia.

DEATH AT A DANCE

Cold Case File ?

*Sniff hall, owned by Lon Sniff, First and Fir,
Deer Trail. The dance hall was on the second
floor. The saloon was closed because of prohibi-
tion and Sniff hall was torn down in 1930*

Music and the voices and laughter of party goers may have
still been heard coming from the Sniff Hall dance floor as
shots rang out in the parking lot.

On the night of December 23, 1922, Howard Hamilton and
Pearl Coeur were shot by a hidden assassin as they were leaving a
Christmas dance at Sniff Hall in Deer Trail. Mr. Hamilton was killed
instantly with one bullet in the heart. Miss Coeur was shot in the
back and seriously injured. She was rushed to St. Anthony's Hospital
in Denver. Who fired those shots remains a mystery to this day.

Twenty-four year old Howard B. Hamilton, World War I vet-
eran, was the son of a respected merchant and the postmaster of
Buick, Colorado. At the time of the shooting, Hamilton was at-
tending a vocational school in Denver. Hamilton was well liked

and had no known enemies. Pearl Coeur was eighteen and was a switchboard operator in Deer Trail. She lived with her family in Deer Trail, about six blocks from the scene of the murder. She also could not think of anyone who would wish to harm her.

Howard Hamilton
1898-1922

It was at first thought that Howard had shot Pearl and escaped in the dark, as he was perceived to be missing immediately following the shooting. No one had seen him take the first bullet and fall in front of a parked car. Because of the confusion, his body was not discovered for an hour after the shooting.

Witnesses said they had seen only the flash of the gunshot in the dark and a man wearing a gray cap and overcoat run behind the ice house. It was too dark to see any detail. Foot prints were found around the ice house.

Apparently, lacking any clue as to the motive, the investigators decided it must have been jealousy over the attentions of Miss Coeur. During the investigation three suspects were taken in for questioning. Jake Leel, a Union Pacific section hand, who showed up intoxicated, and had shown a lot of attention to Pearl at the dance. He repeatedly asked her and others to dance, and seemed peeved that he was always turned down. He demanded that the management force Pearl and the other young ladies to dance with him. Instead, he was asked to leave.

George Griffith, thirty years old, from Carthage, Illinois, who was a friend of the Coeur family, had been visiting at the Coeur home for a few weeks. Griffith's sister was married to Mr. Coeur's brother, and they lived in Ferris, Ill. George had come to Colorado to conclude some business between Mr. Coeur and his brother. George spent a lot of his time, while in Deer Trail, at the phone office visiting with Pearl while she attended the switchboard. Witnesses said Mr. Griffith had left the dance at about 11:30 and appeared to be displeased.

C. E. Lewis, a special deputy, who first came to Deer Trail a few months earlier to investigate charges of bootlegging in the area. He was later arrested and accused of taking checks from Sheriff McNamara's office. Lewis had been friendly with Pearl while in Deer Trail. He had been calling and corresponding with Miss Coeur for a few months. The two were said to quarrel often. Lewis was not in attendance at the dance, and was able to provide an alibi for the time of the shooting.

There was really no evidence against any of the three men, other than a possible weak motive, and eventually Leel and Lewis were released. George Griffith, however, was taken into custody at three a.m. by Deputy Sheriff S. J. Hanks, and charged with second degree murder. He was taken to jail in Littleton wearing the same clothing he had worn at the dance that night, which consisted of a gray serge suit, khaki shirt and colorful neck tie, a dark gray overcoat with gloves in the pockets, and a gray cap. The last two articles became part of the evidence against him.

Griffith said he was not in the vicinity at the time of the shooting, but in fact, had gone home to the Coeur residence, where he sat up and read until 1:30 a.m. There were witnesses willing to testify that he was seen on the stairs of the dance hall fifteen minutes before the murder was committed. Ruby Coeur, Pearl's sister, said she got up between 1:00 and 1:30 a.m. to get a handkerchief, and the house was quiet and dark. Investigators' suspicions were also aroused by Griffith's carefree, almost jesting manner, in light of his good friend just having been shot.

The missing link in the theory that Griffith had done it was, where was the gun? The next morning, a thorough search was organized. A large group of men, walking arm's length apart, searched the area surrounding the scene of the shooting, then expanded to cover about every inch of Deer Trail. They checked rubbish heaps, abandoned wells, and other likely places, hoping to find the .38 caliber revolver used in the murder, or any other clues. Nothing was found.

Police also pursued a theory that the bootlegger gang that Lewis had run out of the country earlier, was somehow involved in the killing. They may have been after Lewis and thought he would be escorting Pearl. This was further bolstered by two witnesses who swore they had seen a large enclosed touring car speeding away from the dance hall immediately after the shooting. Tire tracks were found between Sniff Hall and the West End Garage, where no one would ordinarily park, and they had spun out as if leaving in a hurry. Also, witnesses said that a car fitting that description had been seen in Deer Trail two weeks before the shooting. The two men in the car were seen talking to Pearl Coeur in front of the telephone office. However, no specific suspects or connection to the bootleggers was ever found.

1923 newspaper
photograph of Pearl Coeur

After spending over two weeks in the hospital, Pearl Coeur returned home and told what little she could recall about the incident. She said that she, her mother and father, and George Griffith attended a picture show that evening at the Crystal Theater above Sniff Hall. After the show, her parents returned home and she and Griffith remained for the dance. After she met Howard Hamilton at the dance, she spent the rest of the evening with him. She had known Howard for several years, but had not seen or talked to him since last year when she was a senior at North Denver High School and he was doing vocational work.

As she and Howard were leaving the dance, walking along side by side toward his car which was parked against the icehouse, sixty yards to the rear of the dance hall. Howard was hit by the first shot, coming from in front of them. She did not remember seeing the flash of the gun, so she could not say for sure where the shot came from. Then she thought she must have turned to run and the second shot hit her in the back. She said that after the shooting, no one was thinking straight. Some of the boys quickly took her home. Before her parents took her to the hospital, she remembered seeing George Griffith there. He seemed cool and unconcerned and was fully dressed, not like he had just gotten out of bed.

She also told that C. E. Lewis became a friend of her family while he was in Deer Trail and because of that, he had kept her from being arrested when she was accused of being involved in the bootlegging ring. She added that the whole bootlegging thing was ludicrous, she had nothing to do with bootlegging and they would have no reason to shoot her or Howard. About three months after Pearl's release from the hospital, she and her parents moved to Boulder.

George Griffith's brother and two uncles, both attorneys, came from Illinois and Idaho to help with his defense. They claimed to have the evidence that would acquit George, but were unable to get a hearing in court. In February, the prosecution still did not have sufficient evidence to take the case to trial. The Griffith family took their case to the State Supreme Court in March, asking that charges be dropped due to lack of evidence. The Supreme Court ruled that George would have to remain in jail and stand trial, set for October. Finally, on July 16, after spending over six months in jail with no hearing, George Griffith's case was taken before the Arapahoe County Grand Jury.

The grand jury was in session ten days and heard forty-six witnesses in a fruitless effort to solve the mystery of the case. The verdict was that George Griffith be forthwith discharged from custody and released, and that the indictment against him be marked "Not a true bill." Griffith immediately left with his lawyers amid rumors of lawsuits arising out of his lengthy confinement in jail.

A lawsuit was indeed filed by Griffith's Attorneys in the amount of $84,400, against Robert McNamara, former Arapahoe County Sheriff, W. L. Boatwright, District Attorney, Deputy Sheriffs S. J. Hanks, Paul Smith, and William Kingsbury, and other Deer Trail residents. Damages stated in the suit were, "false, malicious and unwarranted arrest, damage and defamation of character, and physical impairment." Results of that suit are not known.

It is also unknown to what degree the murder investigation continued, but no further arrests were ever made and the murder was never solved.

Resources: Deer Trail Tribune - Dec. 29, 1922, Jan. 5, 1923; Littleton Independent - Dec. 29, 1922, July 13, 1923, July 27, 1923, Aug. 3, 1923, August 24, 1923; Haswell Herald - Aug. 2, 1923; Rocky Mt. News – Dec. 25, 26, 27, 28, 29, 30, 31, 1922, May 23, 1948; Denver Post – Dec. 25, 26, 27, 28, 29, 1922; Colorado Springs Gazette – Dec. 25, 1922.

LAMAR BANK ROBBERY

First Crime Solved By Single Print

Although the notorious Fleagle gang had a history of bank robberies in the early 1900s, probably most of the people of Lamar, Colorado, had never heard of them until they came to town on May 23, 1928.

The Fleagle family raised four boys on a farm near Garden City, Kansas. The two older boys were hard working and conscientious. But Ralph and William "Jake" became involved in drinking and gambling, which soon escalated to bank robbery. Historians estimate they may have been responsible for sixty percent of 1920's heists in Kansas and California. They would return home with money and tell their folks they made it in the stock market. They soon rented their own ranch at Marienthal, Kansas, near Scott City. It was known as a horse ranch, but had no horses. It was used as a 'front' and a rendezvous for the Fleagle boys.

It was from this ranch that Jake and Ralph Fleagle planned their assault on the First National Bank of Lamar. They made the six hour drive many times to case the bank and study the layout. They obtained maps of roads in Prowers County and planned their getaway. Jake decided it was a job for no less than four men, so they recruited George Abshier and Howard "Heavy" Royston. Abshier was an oil driller and gambler and Royston was an engineer in a cement plant in San Andreas, California. They had probably worked with the Fleagle brothers before.

The four heavily armed men left the Kansas ranch at three a.m. driving a blue 1927 Buick Master Six, and in possession of license plates from Colorado, Kansas, Oklahoma, and California to throw off pursuers.

They entered the Lamar bank at 1:00 p.m. on May 23, 1928. With guns in hand, they shouted for everyone to get their "hands up." In the noise and confusion of the moment, Bank President A. N. Parrish ducked back into his office and got a .45 he had hidden there. From the door of his office he fired at the closest robber. His shot hit Heavy Royston in the jaw, and then by all accounts, all hell broke loose as bullets began to fly. In the melee, Mr. Parrish was hit and killed. Juddo Parrish, the son of the president, was also a bank employee, and was killed coming to his father's aide. Other employees and customers got down on the floor and avoided the bullets.

The robbers loaded the contents of the bank's vault, - around ten thousand in cash, twelve thousand in Liberty Bonds, and two hundred thousand in commercial paper, - into pillow cases and grabbed two hostages and made their exit out the back door. They had originally planned to take Juddo Parrish as hostage because they believed the bank president would not pursue them at the risk of his son's life. Since Juddo had been killed they took Edward Lundgren, a one armed teller, and another teller named Everett Kesinger.

Sheriff L. E. Alderman of Lamar was soon in pursuit of the bank robbers. The high speed car chase ended at a crossing of Sand Creek northeast of Lamar after the robbers used rifles to disable the sheriff's vehicle. Not too far after that the gang released Lundgren. Kesinger asked to be released also because he had a wife and new baby, but the bandits would not listen. They kept him on the running board of the car as a shield.

When they arrived back at the Kansas ranch at nightfall, Royston, who had been shot in the face was in need of medical attention. They got Dr. W. W. Wineinger, from nearby Dighton,

133

Kansas, to come to the ranch by telling him that a boy's foot had been crushed by a tractor. Even though he'd been tricked, Dr. Wineinger treated Royston. Then the gang tied the doctor up, blindfolded him, and took him away from the ranch and shot him in the back of the head. They rolled him off into a ravine north of Scott City, Kansas, and drove his Hudson Automobile in after him. The Fleagle brothers then took Kesinger to a shack near Liberal, Kansas and shot him. The body was not discovered until about three weeks after the bank robbery.

The gang divided the cash and some of the bonds. They later told that they burned the rest. They split up and scattering all over the country. Abshire took Royston to Minnesota to see a dental surgeon, and then went to Grand Junction, Colorado. Royston later returned home to San Andreas, California. Ralph and Jake traveled separately from California to Illinois.

In the fifteen month nationwide man hunt that followed, five other criminals were arrested as suspects in the robbery. W. J. "Whitey" Walker, wanted for murder in several states, was extradited by Gov. Franklin Roosevelt from New York to Colorado in connection to the case. Charles Clinton and Ely Mace were arrested in Kansas City. Rosendo Dorames was arrested in Las Angeles. Floyd Jarrett was positively identified by seven witnesses from within the bank, as a member of the bank robbing gang.

Posses and search parties combed the area along the Colorado-Kansas border for the gang or clues to their whereabouts. A Colorado National Guard airplane, helping with the search, spotted Dr. Wineinger's car in the ravine. After finding the body and processing the car, a single fingerprint was found on the window of Dr. Wineinger's car. The fingerprint was sent to the Bureau of Investigation in Washington D.C. Because finger printing was in its early stages of crime investigation, it took thirteen months to track down the owner of the print. When it was discovered that it belonged to Jake Fleagle, who had served a term in the Oklahoma State Penitentiary, an APB was put out nationwide for the Fleagle gang. This was a landmark case for the soon to be FBI because it was the first case where a single finger print was used to solve a crime.

The first Fleagle's to be arrested were the honest hard working brothers, Fred and Walt, and father, Jacob, on their Garden City farm. There, police also found an address for Ralph Fleagle in Kankakee, Illinois, where he was arrested in August 1929. After several weeks in jail, Ralph finally agreed to confess in exchange for the release of his innocent family members. He was also told they would waive the death penalty if he revealed the identities of the rest of the gang, which he did.

Very soon after Ralph's confession, George Abshier (a.k.a. Bill Messick) was arrested in Grand Junction and Howard Royston in San Andreas, California. All three were charged with first degree murder, robbery, and kidnapping. The man hunt continued for Jake who remained at large. Abshier and Royston also eventually confessed, but probably out of retaliation against Ralph selling them out, they blamed all the killing on Ralph and Jake.

In October 1929, trials for the three men began in Prowers County District Court. Since all three men had confessed, most of the arguments in court were over the death penalty sentence. In the end all three men were found guilty and sentenced to hang. Appeals were taken to the Supreme Court in May 1930, and they were denied in June. On July 16, 1930, Ralph Fleagle, age fifty, was hanged at the Colorado State Penitentiary at Canon City. Abshier and Royston, both thirty-four years old, were hanged on July 18.

At this time, Jake Fleagle was hiding in the Ozark Mountains using the name William Harrison. Although, it appears that he had not been there the entire two years. He was the chief suspect in a Southern Pacific passenger train robbery in Pittsburg, California in June 1929, and was wanted for numerous California Post Office robberies around that same time.

Jake, reading about the verdicts in the Colorado trials, wanted to do something to save his brother Ralph. On July 6, 1930,

William Harrison (Jake) wrote a letter to Colorado Governor W. H. Adams pleading for clemency for Ralph Fleagle. Handwriting in the letter was compared to that of Jake Fleagle because of the odd way he made a capital "D." The handwriting matched and tied Jake to the area in the Ozarks where the letter was mailed. As they closed in, nearly twenty police agencies from various states where Jake was wanted became involved. They placed ads in several Ozark newspapers regarding a meeting of his confederates to discuss contemplated bank robberies in Indiana and Illinois. Then they waited and watched.

On October 14, 1930, Jake Fleagle boarded a Missouri Pacific train at Branson, Missouri to attend that meeting. Many officers were aboard that train waiting for Jake. They called for him to stop and put his hands up. Instead, Jake went for his gun. An officer fired and hit Jake. Jake died of this wound the following morning.

Resources: Eagle Valley Enterprise, June 22, 1928, Apr. 5, 1929; Record Journal Douglas County, Feb. 1, 1929, Apr. 19, 1929, Aug. 9, 1929, Oct. 25, 1929; Steamboat Pilot, Aug. 23, 1929, Aug. 30, 1929, May 21, 1930, June 20, 1930; Fleagle Gang, Wikipedia; Appleton Post Crescent, Appleton, Wisconsin, Aug. 30,1929, October 1, 1929; Reno Evening Gazette, Reno, Nevada, Oct. 5, 1929, Oct. 15, 1929; Havre Daily News Promoter, Havre, Montana, Oct. 6, 1929, Oct. 9, 1929; Greeley Daily Tribune, Oct. 14, 1930;The Iola Register, Iola, Kansas, Oct. 14, 1930; Springfield Leader, Springfield, Missouri, Oct. 15, 1930; Chillicothe Constitution Tribune, Chillicothe, Missouri, Oct. 15, 1930.

MURDER WITH NO PROVOCATION

Deer Trail Rancher Killed

*James Ambrose Scott about
1914*

Park County authorities called it one of the strangest cases in the history of Colorado crime annals, a murder apparently without a motive.

The victim was James Ambrose Scott, a sixty-seven year old rancher from Deer Trail, who was working at a resort in Singleton, Colorado, between Grant and Bailey, where the murder occurred. The killer was Robert L. Proudfoot a twenty-seven year old sheep man also from Deer Trail.

Proudfoot, along with a friend, William Murray, drove up to Singleton Resort on Wednesday, June 15, 1932, to visit their old friend, Jim Scott. They waited at the resort and greeted Scott when he returned from a horseback ride. After a short while, Proudfoot excused himself and went to an outbuilding. Then Murray and Scott began chatting about fishing. Scott took Murray to a milk-house to show him some rainbow trout he had recently caught.

Jim Scott was standing on a stool, his back to the door, lifting a pan-full of fish from the top of the icebox when Proudfoot entered. Without a word Proudfoot stepped close behind Scott, drew a revolver, held it not more than two feet from Scott's head and pulled the trigger. He then pocketed the pistol and walked out.

Mrs. Scott came running when she heard the shot. As she met Proudfoot she asked what had happened. Proudfoot replied "You ought to know." Mrs. Scott asked, "Has something happened to my husband?" Proudfoot told her, "Yes, I shot him."

Proudfoot and Murray drove away as Mrs. Scott and other ranch employees tended to Jim, who did not die immediately, but never regained consciousness. The resort manager called the police and road blocks were set up. When Proudfoot came to the road block he stopped and readily admitted that he had shot Scott.

Jim Scott was born in Ohio in 1865. At age twenty-one Jim headed west. He encountered a cattle drive in Nebraska and signed on as cook's helper. The owner of the herd was C. B. Rhodes, the future owner of the White Ranch at Deer

Trail. Scott was trading horses in Julesburg, Colorado where he became the first sheriff of Sedgewick County in 1886. In 1891, he married Henrietta Wamsley. They moved to Deer Trail where six sons were born. Jim continued in the horse business, and after his marriage ended in divorce, raised his six sons with the help of housekeepers.

In 1908, Jim married the schoolmarm, Jeannette Aukema, and they had two children. The size of his ranch increased over the years. He also partnered with his sister, Laura Pankake, on a sheep ranch eight miles southwest of Deer Trail. They would ship their sheep by narrow-gauge railroad up to Grant in the summer where they grazed above timberline. The ewes were driven back to Deer Trail in the fall by Mexican sheepherders.

The depression of the 1930s caused a drop in prices of lambs and wool and about everything else. This caused Jim to lose most of his land, and he was forced to take a job as a manager and guide at the Singleton resort near Bailey, Colorado. This was Jim's first job working for someone else since his early days in Colorado. His wife, Jeannette cooked at the resort. This was also her first employment since Jim took her out of the classroom.

Robert Proudfoot lived with his brother, Jim, on a sheep ranch southwest of Deer Trail. He had, at one time, taken care of a band of sheep for Jim Scott. They had been friends for years and no one knew of any harsh words or hard feelings between the two men.

Immediately after the shooting, Proudfoot was taken to jail in Fairplay. Deputy Sheriff Adolph Christopher of Bailey, said that Proudfoot readily admitted shooting Scott declaring, "He ruined my life." Robert Proudfoot was charged with the murder by a coroner's jury at Fairplay, and a sanity examination was ordered. At the hearing Proudfoot stated, "Scott was ruining my moral character and talking about me."

William Murry, also a Deer Trail rancher, was held for questioning. Proudfoot absolved Murray of any knowledge of, or any part in the murder, and Murray was released.

Jim Scott was a well known and well liked rancher at Deer Trail and the surrounding area. He had no known enemies. Jim Scott's funeral was held in the Deer Trail school gymnasium with a very large attendance of family and friends, and very moving eulogies were given by his associates. He was buried in Evergreen Cemetery in Deer Trail.

Robert Proudfoot was eventually declared insane and sent to the Colorado State Hospital in Pueblo where he died in the 1940s.

Resources: Rocky Mountain News, June 24, 1932, June 25, 1932; Treasured Memories, Deer Trail Pioneer Historical Society, 1990.

AGATE RANCHER MURDERED IN HIS SLEEP

Motive is a Mystery

Jim Jolly, prominent Agate rancher, was shot and killed during an apparent robbery at his ranch home, six miles east of Agate, Colorado, on December 10, 1980. On the night of the murder, the three occupants of the ranch house were seventy-seven year old ranch owner, James B. Jolly, his housekeeper Jessie Dumcum, and her young granddaughter. Jim's wife, Katherine, was in the nursing home at the time.

Mrs. Dumcum was awakened late that evening by pounding on the door. The housekeeper got up and went to the door, and two men wearing ski masks, and both armed with hand guns, forced their way in and demanded money. She was ordered to take the men to Mr. Jolly's room. The two men woke up Jolly and asked, "Where is it, the safe and the money?" Jolly had no time to answer, he barely made a sound and one of the robbers shot him as he lay in his bed, the bullet directed upward from under his chin, killing him instantly.

The men then told the housekeeper she, too, would be shot if she didn't come up with some money. They were quoted as saying, "We know you've got a lot of coins and money and a safe. They told us you have a lot of money." The men found money in Jim's wallet and Mrs. Dumcum's purse amounting to

141

between seven and eight hundred dollars, and stole three rifles and a pistol. They bound the housekeeper's hands and feet and fled.

Mrs. Dumcum's granddaughter, who stayed safely hidden in another room, and was unharmed, untied her grandmother. Mrs. Dumcum could not call for help, as the murderers had yanked out the telephone. She then discovered they had also disabled the ranch vehicles by letting the air out of the tires. She found one old pickup that they had missed, and drove it to Agate and called the Elbert County Sheriff.

Jim Jolly was the son of John and Jane Jolly. He was born April 4, 1903, the seventh of eleven children and third of six sons. Jim's father, John Jolly, came to the Deer Trail area from Scotland in 1887. After establishing his homestead, he went back to Scotland and returned with his bride, Jane, in 1891.

Jim learned the ranching business growing up and working on the family sheep ranch east of Deer Trail. He also learned to run a business by managing the Jolly Mercantile Store in Deer Trail, as each of the Jolly boys did in turn. Jim acquired his Agate ranch in the early 1930s and built it into one of the largest cattle and sheep ranches in Elbert County, consisting of 32,000 acres. In 1934, he married Katherine Fulford, fondly known as 'Mina'. They had no children.

A break in the murder case came early, only two days after the crime. Two men, Thomas Eugene Payseno, 37, and Charles Richard Bayles, 25, were arrested in Denver for questioning. A female informant had come forward. She had apparently met Payseno earlier at the Colorado State Penitentiary while visiting another prisoner. Payseno had just been released from prison the day before the murder. The informant met Payseno and Bayles in a bar on December 11, the day following the murder. Payseno told her that "he had killed a guy last night at a house about 60 miles east of Denver." Payseno bragged that he was a hit man and had been hired to kill the man.

From this time forward, mystery surrounded the case. Almost immediately the court issued a gag order, and as the investigation continued, all court documents were sealed. The Denver newspapers fought these orders, but the courts would not budge. On April 10, three more men were arrested, Charles Austin Turner and Donald Jack Priest both of Denver, and Charles Edward Saxton of Ogallala, Nebraska. They were charged with first-degree murder, aggravated robbery and criminal conspiracy, and the judge in the case sealed the arrest affidavits, stating "something new had come up." Prosecutors stated that they might seek charges of pre-meditated murder, suggesting that they believed that Jolly's death was planned and the robbery was just a cover up, but they gave no other details.

It was presumed that both Charles Saxton and Charles Bayles turned States evidence as they were both seen in court wearing bullet proof vests. Because of testimony given by Saxton, Charles Richard "Bud" Lee was arrested April 25. Saxton also told that planning for the robbery had begun early in November. He said they made several trips to the ranch, to get the layout of the place, after Bud Lee told him that Jolly had at least $100,000 in his house. On one trip, Saxton said Jolly asked them what they were doing there. They made an excuse and left. On a second trip, Jolly chased the intruders away by firing a gun, after telling them to "get the hell out of there."

It is believed that some of these suspects met in the penitentiary. Payseno, Bayles, Turner, and Priest all served various lengths of overlapping time during the seventies. On May 1, a seventh suspect was arrested, Thomas Hutton of Denver. His only connection seemed to be, that he was a resident of the same apartment building where two of the other suspects resided.

Saxton and Bayles, because of their cooperation with authorities, plea bargained and received two years in prison. Turner, Priest, and Lee pled guilty to lesser charges and presumably also received light sentences, the lengths of these are unknown. Charges against Hutton were later dropped.

In March of 1982, Payseno pled guilty to charges of first-degree murder, aggravated robbery, and theft. Five other charges against him were dropped. The guilty plea to the murder charge enabled Payseno to avoid the death penalty. He was given a mandatory life sentence with no possibility of parole for twenty years for the murder charge, plus twenty-four years for the other two charges. Because Payseno pled guilty, no trial was held, therefore, no more information about his "hit-man" statement, or the prosecutor's "robbery cover-up" theory ever came out in court testimony. Thomas Payseno was sent to the Colorado State Penitentiary, (for at least the second time), he will be eligible for parole in August of 2014, at the age of seventy.

Jim Jolly's funeral was held at the Agate School with a huge crowd in attendance. He was buried at Riverside Cemetery in Fort Morgan, Colorado. Jim was a well known and well liked Colorado rancher. He was an active member of the Elbert County Livestock Association, the Colorado and National Cattlemen's Associations, and the Colorado and National Wool Growers Associations. He was a charter member of the First Baptist Church of Deer Trail. He was a lifelong Republican and a committeeman in the Agate precinct for many years. He was appointed to the panel to select District Judges, and served in the Colorado House of Representatives in the 1950s.

He and his wife took an active interest in the youth of Colorado. They sponsored calves for the 4-H catch-it-contest, financed numerous students' college educations, and helped the Agate school in many ways. They showed their abundant kindness and generosity to many people in the area. In later years when Jim would visit his wife in the nursing home, he would take some kind of treats or gifts for all the residents. The Jim Jolly Memorial Scholarship Fund was set up in his memory.

Resources: Denver Post Dec. 11, 1980, Dec. 12, 1980, Dec. 12, 1980, Dec. 13, 1980, Dec. 16, 1980, Dec. 18, 1980, Rocky Mt. News April 10, 1981, April 25, 1981, May 1, 1981, March 10, 1982; Colorado State Penitentiary.

COLORADO NEWS BRIEFS

Rocky Mountain News – Dec. 20, 1870

SHOOTING AT RIVER BEND

December 19th at 6:00 p.m. River Bend was the scene of quite a lively shooting affair. M.M. Downin, better known as "Waspie," and Tom Carson, exchanged some seven or eight shots, which, however, did no serious damage. Carson received two slight flesh wounds, and Downin has several bullet holes in his coat. Then everything quieted down. But both are renowned western men, and there is reason to believe there will be more fun before the matter is ended. Downin took the train for Hugo at 6:45.

Rocky Mountain News – May 11, 1871

MAN SHOT AT RIVER BEND

A soldier named Ward went into a saloon in River Bend on May 10, 1871 and wanted to pawn his overcoat for whiskey. The proprietor, J. F. Dugan refused this proposition. Ward became abusive and wanted to fight. This accomplished nothing except getting him thrown out. Ward went home after his rifle, and came back and tried to get back in the saloon. When this failed, he called

Dugan to come out and fired a shot into the saloon. Dugan went out with his Winchester. When Ward saw him he raised his rifle to his shoulder. Dugan anticipated his intent and fired first. Ward was hit a few inches above the heart. This happened at 1:00 p.m. At 4:00 p.m. Ward died. Dugan went to Hugo to give himself up to the authorities, but could find none. He will probably have to go to Denver to surrender.

Denver Daily Times – Oct. 6, 1873

AN EXCITING TRIP

The passengers who came in over the Kansas Pacific yesterday thought they had an exciting trip across the plains. The sheriff of Hays had ridden the train to Wallace, Kansas in pursuit of Tom Irwin, a noted outlaw wanted for many crimes. As the sheriff got off the train, he saw Irwin in a saloon with a revolver in one hand and a knife in the other. The sheriff covered him with his rifle and ordered him to throw down his weapons and put up his hands, which he did. After the cuffs were on, other men in the saloon became rowdy and a gun accidently discharged inflicting a minor wound to another patron, who set up a howl.

The passengers on the train who had witnessed this were excited and some were frightened. One lady in particular, who was coming west to join her husband, was sure they would all be killed. When the train stopped at River Bend, Colorado the lady commented that everyone there had a rifle or revolver or two or three of them. At Bijou they met a special train containing volunteers. These men were thoroughly armed, which also frightened the lady. The conductor told her not to worry about it, because all men in Colorado had a couple of revolvers stuck in their belt because it was the custom of the country. She declared that if she found her husband dressed in that manner she would divorce him.

Las Animas Leader - January 12, 1877

CLAY ALLISON'S LAST GUNFIGHT

Clay Allison was a well known gunfighter who built his reputation in Texas and New Mexico in the 1870s. He was also well
known for causing trouble in Southeastern Colorado towns such
as Trinidad. The killing that probably did the most for his notori-
ety took place in Las Animas, Colorado.

On December 21, 1876, Clay Allison and his brother John
traveled from their home in Cimarron, New Mexico to Las
Animas and were on a drinking spree at the Olympic Dance
Hall. Bent County Sheriff, John Spiers had been alerted that
they were in town. The Allison's had caused trouble there in the
past. When the Allison's started trouble, Deputy Sheriff Charles
Faber went to the Olympic and asked the Allison brothers to
check their guns. They flatly refused and continued to make
trouble.

Faber left but soon returned with a double barreled shotgun
and two other deputies. When Faber entered, Clay was at the bar
and John was at the end of the hall dancing. With little warning,
Faber fired at John who was hit three times. Clay returned fire,
pumping several rounds into the deputy. The other two deputies
fled, with Clay in hot pursuit, but he soon gave up the chase and
returned to see to his injured brother.

Deputy Faber died at the scene. John eventually recovered
from his injuries. John and Clay were both arrested for manslaugh-
ter but were eventually found not guilty because of self defense,
because Faber shot first with no warning.

Shortly after this incident Clay Allison married, had two children and settled down on a ranch near Pecos, Texas. Ironically,
he died in a freak accident in 1887. He was hauling a wagon

load of supplies to his ranch when a sack of feed slid off the load, Allison tried to catch it. He fell under the wagon and the heavy load passed over his head and neck. His favorite saying is carved on his tombstone, "Never killed a man that did not need killing."

COLORADO LIVESTOCK REPORT

Colorado Weekly Chieftan, (Pueblo) – January 11, 1877

Following are the rates on livestock shipped to Kansas City after January 1, 1877. From Cheyenne, Greeley, Evans, Denver, Colorado Springs, Pueblo, Deer Trail, and River Bend - $75 per car load, from Hugo - $72, from Las Animas and Kit Carson - $70. Double-decker cars for sheep will be furnished for an additional $10 per car.

Denver Daily Tribune – January 1, 1878; Colorado Springs Gazette – April 13, 1878

The 1877 export of cattle was the largest ever to date. Shipped over the Kansas Pacific Railway from Denver, Deer Trail, River Bend, and Hugo was 1,486 car loads, or about 29,720 head. When added to shipments on the Atchison, Topeka & Santa Fe, the total was 2,972 cars or 59,440 head, Union Pacific estimates 15,000 head. This gives a total of 74,400 head with an average of $35 per head. Total value of Colorado cattle shipments for 1877 was $2,605,400. Per head totals were: Denver 8,140 (includes those coming through Denver from the Denver Pacific); Deer Trail 10,820; Hugo 6,080; Kit Carson 1,410; Arroya 800.

Fairplay Flume – October 18, 1883

From the best information that could be had we have ascertained that the cattle along the line of the Kansas Pacific are owned as follows:

Mr. F. P. Ernest, whose home ranch is at Deer Trail, his cattle number 30,000 head. W. H. H. Cranmer 25,000 head. The John Hittson herd, whose home ranch is at Deer Trail, 15,000 head. Henry Gebbhard 6 to 8,000 head. Mssrs. Tucker & Wilson, Denver parties, 7 to 8,000 head. W. H. Metcalf, also Denver representative, 10,000 head. Mssrs. Holt & Co. 15,000.

Colorado Springs Gazette – March 23, 1878

DEATH BY A HUSBAND'S NEGLECT

A cowboy passing through Bijou Basin found the body of a woman who had apparently frozen to death in the recent storm. She was only a few yards from a nearby shanty. She had a baby, ten months old in her arms, and another child, about three years old, was buried in snow a few feet away.

The herder went to the neighbors for help. The woman was identified as Mrs. Reed, who had been living in the shanty with her family for a few months. In checking the shanty, they discovered that it was so poorly constructed that there was about two feet of snow inside. There was no fire wood except a few sticks in the stove, which Mrs. Reed evidently tried to kindle, but also no matches were found. Mrs. Reed was not wearing a coat and there was very little bedding and no food found in the cabin. Mrs. Reed must have decided that in her hopeless situation, her only hope was to go for help.

It was discovered that Mr. Reed, who had recently got a job at Feasel's mill, was at Bijou Basin on a drunken spree, only a few miles from his home. The community was outraged that a man could leave his family cold, starving and in such poor conditions during a storm while he spent his pay on whiskey.

Fearing the indignation of his neighbors, Mr. Reed tried to escape but the coroner ordered his arrest for murder by neglect. He is now confined to jail, but feelings are so strong that he is afraid that he may be lynched.

Leadville Chronicle – March 1879

STAGE COACH ROBBERY

In 1879, there had been a rash of stage coach robberies along the old stage road between Buena Vista and Leadville. It appeared to be the same robber each time and he only hit the coaches carrying large gold shipments, even though these shipments were supposed to be secret.

Sheriff Kirkham came up with a secret plan to outwit the bandit. He did not tell the stage company, his deputies, or anyone about the plan. The sheriff, dressed as a female passenger, was aboard the March 7th stage which was carrying a gold shipment from a mine in Leadville. Just as he suspected, about ten miles south of Twin Lakes Junction, the robber stepped out onto the road brandishing his weapons and ordered the driver to stop.

Sheriff Kirkham quietly tore off his disguise, drew his weapon on the bandit and ordered him to drop his gun and put his hands up. Instead the robber fled with weapon in hand. The Sheriff shot the bandit and he fell dead.

The greatest surprise came when the sheriff turned the body over and discovered it was his wife dressed as a man. The Sheriff was so ashamed and embarrassed that he buried his wife right where she was killed along the stage road.

151

The granite tombstone, which is still on the other side of the river at Twin Lakes Junction, reads: My wife – Jane Kirkham, Died March 7, 1879, Aged 38 years, 3 months, 7 days.

Fort Morgan Times – May 20, 1892

A MYSTERIOUS DEATH

May 16, 1892, D. A. Snyder, who lives eighteen miles south of Fort Morgan, reported to Coroner Putnam that his neighbor and brother-in-law, John Pflager, had committed suicide. Coroner Putnam summoned a jury of six men, and accompanied also by Dr. Balfour and Sheriff Dingman, they went to the scene to investigate.

On arrival, the deceased was found lying on the remains of a bed in a natural position. His stomach and extremities and most of the bed, had been consumed by fire. The doctor found no evidence of a gunshot, even though a gun was found near the bed. There were bruises around the neck that could indicate strangulation. There was also no explanation why nothing else in the dugout was burned. The jury ruled that since it would not be possible to strangle oneself, and that he would have had to be already dead or unconscious to be consumed by fire, that he died of unknown causes inflicted by an unknown person with felonious intent.

John Pflager had been living south of Fort Morgan for about four years and was a thriving stock raiser. He was living by himself in a dugout. At the present time, his wife and children were in Hickman, Nebraska, so the children could attend school. Neighbors testified that he had been acting strange lately. He was thought, at times, by some to be insane. He had been telling that he was receiving threatening letters and someone was trying to kill him, and that someone was giving him medicine with poison in it.

With so little evidence and no other information, the murder was never solved. John Pflager was buried on the prairie near the scene of his death in case there was a possibility of a solution of the mystery. A lone tombstone remains.

Rocky Mountain News – Aug. 31, 1881

WORK OF THE LIGHTNING

Noah Cann, employer of Thomas M. Douglass, the man who was killed by lightning near Deer Trail a few days ago, has found several coins, consisting of several silver dollars, a twenty cent piece, several cents, etc., belonging to the dead ranch hand, and brought them in to the coroner. Little scraps of clothing were also scattered all around the place where Douglass met his death. The heavy silver watch chain belonging to the deceased has never been found.

Rocky Mountain News – Aug. 5, 1900

FARMER KILLED BY LIGHTNING

At 5 o'clock last night, while Thomas Robertson and Thomas Moran were putting up hay, four miles south of Deer Trail, a sudden thunderstorm passed over. They took cover under a tree. A bolt of lightning struck both men, killing Robertson instantly and knocking Moran senseless. Robertson came originally from North Carolina. Moran recovered. Coroner McGovern received word of the tragedy and left last night to hold an inquest.

Castle Rock Journal – June 7, 1907

LIGHTNING KILLS YOUTH

Byers, Colo. - While herding a small bunch of ewes and lambs, Mark Allen was struck by lightning and instantly killed. Mark was working for G. A. Snow, a wealthy ranchman whose ranch is three miles south of Byers. When the storm started, Mr. Snow started out to help the boy in with the sheep. When he got within three hundred yards of Allen he saw the lightning strike him down. The boy was thirteen years old and the son of George W. Allen, a ranchman living one mile from Byers.

Aspen Daily Times – January 31, 1909

MAN WANTED FOR MURDER CAUGHT AFTER TWELVE YEAR HUNT

After twelve years, during which time he had traveled over most of the United States, Charles Herndon, wanted in Kentucky for the murder of his wife, has been captured by Denver detectives at Byers, Colorado. The police officers went to Byers last week and, disguised as duck hunters, lay in wait for an opportunity to arrest Herndon.

Herndon is 48 years old and has two daughters. He had been married twice. He learned that his second wife was receiving attentions from other men. He claimed that when he confronted her he had a revolver to frighten her and that it accidently exploded and killed his wife. He was afraid no one would believe it was an accident so he skipped the country and has been on the run since.

Last year he took up a homestead at Byers under the name of Howard.

Steamboat Pilot – January 24, 1912

WOOLEY WILL QUIT ON SHEEP BUSINESS

George D. Wooley, sheep raiser of Moffat county, has given up attempts to raise sheep and is seriously considering moving to a community where there is no strife between sheep men and cattlemen. Ninety-five of his sheep were killed on December 2.

Wooley says that the slaughter of his sheep was in the nature of a warning, not only to himself, but to others. It was done, he believes to discourage him from shipping 2,000 head of sheep from Deer Trail to the Craig neighborhood. He had them on the cars and ready to move when he got word of the slaughter. The 2,000 head are still in Deer Trail.

Wooley says that there are several large cattle companies around Craig that have made up their minds that they are going to keep sheep off the range. They claim that cattle and sheep cannot graze on the same ground.

Wet Mountain Tribune – June 13, 1924

TROUBLE ON THE TRAIN

A band of twenty-five hoboes attempted to overpower the conductor and brakeman on an eastbound Union Pacific freight train near Deer Trail. They were only frustrated in their attempt to gain control of the train when they reached Limon and were overpowered in a battle with Sheriff A. G. Loss and a posse. Nine of the band were placed under arrest and locked in a cattle car until they reached Hugo where they were taken to jail.

Rocky Mountain News – March 16, 1885

DEER TRAIL DANCE

A mistaken idea is prevalent in some portions of the county that the people of Colorado are destitute of refinement, and some persons at the state capital foolishly question the social status of residents of the rural districts. Such doubters would have been led to change their opinions if they had attended a social party at the noted cattle and sheep center, Deer Trail, on Friday evening last.

It was Representative Hodge's dance. Upwards of a hundred ladies and gentlemen were gathered from the surrounding ranches and country, and in point of demeanor, dress, social amenities and acquaintance with the Terpsichorean art, were the peers of people anywhere, East or West.

Deer Trail is a railroad cattle and sheep shipping station on the Kansas Pacific, fifty-five miles east of Denver, and while, not a largev place, is the center of an extensive cattle section which is one of the richest in the state. The ranchmen are generally wealthy and among the most enterprising of their class, their homes are comfortable and in some cases elegant.

The party had been widely talked about, and in a measure was one of the events of the season for our country cousins. It was held in the village school house and the music was excellent. An excellent supper was served at Mrs. Finley's Deer Trail Hotel.

Noticed among those present were the following gentlemen with their wives – Hon. George F. Hodge, Charles Linton, H. G. Brearley, G. J. Lackey, Guy Morrow, Mrs. Keith, Mrs. Cooper, Mrs. Adams, Misses Alice and Belle Finley, Misses Nellie and Maggie Moore, Misses Norton, Leslie, Lupton, Hancock, Middlemist, and Fanchon, Walter Sherrer, Felix Fitzimmons, William Flannery, Thomas Burt, R. P. Stockton, R. G. Wilson, L. R. Tucker, Ward Tucker, A. C. Patchin, Frank Page, Lee Johns, C. E. Pooler, John Wyatt, R. M. Stevens, A. N. Cantley, Dave Roberts, Jacob Miller, Mr. Smith, and Mr. Weatherby.

Elbert County Banner – July 18, 1902

AGATE DANCE

A most enjoyable dance was had at the Three Ring Ranch, Fourth of July night. Music was furnished by the Agate band, supper by Mrs. A. T. Haynes. The following gentlemen were present with their wives: A. U. Scherrer, C. E. Ginger, D. Sultz, W. E. Cronkhite, Aug. Beuck, Paul Lavlett; the Misses Louise, Josie, and Angele Sherrer, Ella Sherrer, Minnie Gebhard, Hazel Tucker, Annie Bond, Mary Corbin, Carrie Mucker, Emily and Pauline Gebhard and Nellie Walker; Messrs Will Dorte, Carl Swain, Will, Harry, Ivan, and Albert Sherrer, Phelps Buell, Henry and Fred Beuck, Henry Gebhard and Jack Sims. All reported having a very good time.

Victor Daily Record – Apr. 6, 1905; Rocky Mountain News – Apr. 12, 1905

MARTIN O'CONNOR THE VICTIM OF FOUL PLAY

On April 6, 1905, Julia O'Connor Deter, of Deer Trail received a telegram informing her that her brother Martin O'Connor of Victor, Colorado, had met an accidental death.

His body had been found at the bottom of a retaining wall near the Gold Coin Mine in Victor, Colorado. It was first thought he may have fallen from the wall. After examination by a coroner's jury, it was determined that his injuries could not have been caused by a fall. Cause of death was ruled to be a crushed skull caused by, from three to five severe blows to the head with a blunt instrument. A two by four was found nearby with O'Connor's hair on it.

Robbery was believed to be the motive because O'Connor, who was a blacksmith at Stratton's Independence Mine, had been paid that day and very little cash was found on the body. Mr. O'Connor was forty-six years old and leaves a widow and three children, ages two, five and seven.

After interviewing witnesses, a search for a miner named Frank Buster began. He was finally arrested in Grand Island, Nebraska in August, 1905. In November, Frank Buster was released and the case against him dismissed when it was determined that there was not enough evidence against him to warrant a trial.

No other arrests were made, and the murder was never solved.

Rocky Mountain News – Sept. 15, 1913

FREE SHAVE OFFERED MAN WHO'LL WED BEFORE CROWD

Deer Trail, Colo., Sept. 14, 1913 – Racing, a ball game, an all-night dance, and a band concert will be among the features of the second annual Deer Trail fair, which will be given next Saturday.

Special inducements will be offered the couple willing to be married before the spectators. The groom will be shaved free, the ceremony will be performed free. An ax, twenty-five pounds of flour, eight pounds of sugar, a pound of coffee, and a pail of lard will be presented to the bride.

Denver Post – Jan. 12, 1915; Rocky Mountain News – Jan. 11, 1915

CRAZED BY HUNGER, WOMAN ATTEMPTS
TO SHOOT DEPUTY

Dora Pitt, alias Mrs. J. Sayer, was arrested at Strasburg, after firing a shot at Arapahoe County Deputy Sheriff D. H. Weaver. Thirty-three year old Pitt said she was crazed with grief, hunger and exposure.

She has three small children in the care of a sister in Nebraska. She has been deserted by her husband and is desperate to provide for herself and her children. Pitt calls herself a spiritual medium, and had been telling fortunes around Strasburg. She was ordered out of Strasburg because she didn't have a license.

When she was contacted by Deputy Weaver, she refused to go. She pulled out a gun and fired at him. She was taken to Littleton to investigate her story and attempt to find her husband.

Evidently something didn't ring true about her story, because she was tried on a charge of assault to kill, found guilty and sentenced to two to five years. She was sent to prison on March 23, 1915, and discharged December 20, 1918.

Denver Post – Sept. 28, 1915; RMN – Oct. 5, 1915; Akron Pioneer – Nov. 12, 1915

FATAL SHOOTING AT BYERS, COLORADO

On Sept. 26, 1915, George Holmden, 78 years old, after losing an argument with 38 year old Dan Bracken, went home and got his double barrel 12-guage shotgun and returned to the scene. He ordered everyone out of the way and shot Bracken in both knees. Witnesses said both men were intoxicated.

Bracken's legs were torn up really bad. In a short time, blood poisoning had set in and one leg was amputated to try to save his life. However, in just over a week, Bracken died of his injuries.

Holmden was held in jail to await trail, which was held in November. He was found guilty of killing Dan Bracken and sentenced to ninety days in jail.

Evidently this 'terrible' sentence did not teach Holmden his lesson. In August of 1916, Holmden, now 79 years old, was found guilty of threatening to kill a man named Buel, at Byers. He was sentenced to six months in jail. This sentence was suspended after Holmden agreed to leave the state.

Denver Post – May 25, 1916

RANCHHAND SHOOTS EMPLOYER

William Kingsbury, a rich cattleman, was shot at his ranch four miles from Deer Trail, by Smith Thompson, who had been a tenant on the ranch for twelve years.

Kingsbury went to the ranch to see about a steam plow. Thompson approached him and said he wanted to talk. Kingsbury was in a hurry and said he would see him some other time. As he turned away, Thompson fired two shots, both hitting Kingsbury in the back. Thompson then turned the gun on himself, placed it just above his heart and fired. The bullet hit a rib and did only slight damage. He was raising the gun to his head to try again, when other ranch employees disarmed him.

Kingsbury was taken to Denver to St. Joseph's Hospital, where he recovered from his wounds.

Kingsbury said he knew of no reason Thompson would want to shoot him.

Thompson said only that it was the outgrowth of an old grudge.

Range Leader, Hugo, CO – April 9, 1921

ROBBER CAUGHT

William W. Prantz, former convict at the Colorado penitentiary, is in jail in Littleton, charged with the robbery of both the Strasburg bank and the railroad depot at Byers. Both crimes were committed in March. When arrested, several railroad tickets, said to have been stolen from the depot at Byers, were found on Prantz.

161

Littleton Independent – Feb. 13, 1920

TWO BOYS GO ON CRIME SPREE

Two Denver boys who are charged with sixteen different crimes, including burglary, larceny, and horse stealing, in Washington, Adams, Jefferson, and Arapahoe Counties, are in the Littleton jail. The prisoners gave their names as Hoot and Floyd Smith, but were later identified as Elmer Day, 15, and David Grove, 16.

They were captured near Deer Trail by a small posse, mounted on horses, led by Deputy Will Kingsbury and Pat Treadwell, a nearby rancher. They followed the trail of the pair from the ranch of George Amon, near Deer Trail, whose house was the latest of many that the boys had ransacked.

When captured, the youths were riding stolen horses with stolen saddles and equipment. They had two revolvers each, one shotgun, and a large quantity of ammunition, all stolen. Many other stolen items were found in the packs on their horses. They both wore red bandana handkerchiefs around their throats in typical "movie" wild west style.

Deer Trail Tribune – Dec. 2, 1932

BOULDER BOY SHOT AS BURGLARY SUSPECT

Jack Brunton, 17, of Boulder, is in serious condition in a Boulder hospital after being shot while fleeing from an alleged burglary in Deer Trail.

As F. T. Snavely and Archie Clark were leaving Ideal Service Station after closing at about 10:30 p.m., they noticed a car parked in front of Tri-Valley Oil station, which was already closed for the night. Being suspicious, they circled around and when they came back by, they saw two men inside the Tri-Valley station. Seeing that they had been discovered, the burglars ran out the back door.

Archie Clark ran next door to the home of Jim Woody and borrowed a shotgun. When he returned, he saw one man running toward Anderson Implement shed. Archie shouted for him to stop, when he did not, Archie fired a shot into the air, since he still did not stop Archie fired another shot, hitting the man in the back.

Doctor Webb was called to give the boy emergency treatment. In the meantime Mr. Snavely and others were searching for the other boy who was found hiding in a hen coop at the rear of the Downen home. He is Joe Gordon, 15, also from Boulder.

The injured boy's father, Mr. L. J. Brunton, is a professor at Colorado State University in Boulder. The boys were runaways and the car they were driving had been stolen in Denver earlier that evening.

The shooting was regretted by Archie, because of the boy's age. However, no one is blaming him, as he had no way to know they were boys, until they were captured. Due to the amount of burglaries that have occurred recently, people felt that he did the right thing in trying to stop them.

The boys were released to the custody of their parents. Jack Brunton did recover from his injuries. What ultimately happened to the boys is unknown.

Made in the USA
Middletown, DE
09 November 2021